Ex-Offenders as Parole Officers

The Parole Officer Aide
Program in Ohio

Joseph E. Scott
The Ohio State University

Lexington Books
D.C. Heath and Company
Lexington, Massachusetts
Toronto   London

Grateful acknowledgment is made for use of material reprinted herein: From Herbert McClosky, "Conservatism and Personality," *American Political Science Review*, Vol. 52, March 1958 (copyright © 1958 American Political Science Review), reprinted by permission; from Rita Volkman and Donald R. Cressey, "Differential Association and the Rehabilitation of Drug Addicts," *American Journal of Sociology*, September 1963 (copyright © 1963 University of Chicago Press), reprinted by permission; from Desmond S. Cartwright and Richard J. Robertson, "Membership in Cliques and Achievement," *American Journal of Sociology*, March 1961 (copyright © 1961, University of Chicago Press), reprinted by permission.

Library of Congress Cataloging in Publication Data

Scott, Joseph E.   1943-
    Ex-offenders as parole officers.

    Bibliography: p.
    Includes index.
    1. Parole—Ohio. 2. Parole officers—Ohio. 3. Paraprofessionals in social service. 4. Ex-convicts—Employment—Ohio. I. Title.
HV9305.02S38   345'.771'077   74-10176
ISBN 0-669-93369-4

Published simultaneously in Canada.

Printed in the United States of America.

International Standard Book Number: 0-669-93369-4

Library of Congress Catalog Card Number: 74-10176

Contents

List of Figures

List of Tables

Acknowledgments

I would like to express my appreciation to several employees of the Adult Parole Authority who facilitated in the data-collection process. Messrs. Ray Gianetta, Nick Gatz, and Ray Capots were very cooperative in allowing access to both records and individuals crucial to the success of the evaluation. Mr. Nick Sanborn, the Parole Officer Aide project director, assisted numerous times in better conceptualizing and understanding some of the problems inherent in such an analysis. The Ohio Adult Parole Authority Unit Supervisors remained helpful throughout the study, and without the cooperation of the many parole officers and parole officer aides who underwent tedious questioning from the research staff, this book could not have been completed.

Several staff members at the Program for the Study of Crime and Delinquency have been most helpful in completing this evaluation. Dr. Harry Allen, Mr. Rick Seiter, and Mr. Jack Baumeister were instrumental in getting the initial contract with the A.P.A. Ms. Ellen Freed and Ms. Fran Simonsen worked out several fiscal problems that were encountered. Pamela Bennett, Greg Barentine, Roger Bennett, Bill Cooper, Dwight Ely, Charles Eden, Harry Fabiano, Thomas Murphy, Pat Snider, Peg Stadler, and Janis Ward assisted in the gathering and coding of the data, and editing and proofreading of the final report. Mike George, Lynne Casterline, and Stu Berry aided in gathering, coding, and analyzing the data, and in preparing rough drafts. Michele Hobbs, Diana Cline, Thea Dinitz, and Jeanette Seeman typed the entire manuscript in one form or another several times. Ms. Judy Tannenbaum contributed her interviewing expertise to the success of the project, and Mr. Dick Haller assisted in doing some of the computer programming. Mr. Roy F. Cromer and his staff at the Research Services Office of the College of Administrative Sciences along with their "MTST" typed each parolee in the first year's sample five personal letters requesting their cooperation and help. Professor Gordon Waldo, Director of the Southeastern Correctional and Criminological Research Center at Florida State University, allowed me to use some of his material in the original questionnaire. To the above people I wish to express my appreciation and thanks.

Special thanks are due Karen Woeste and my wife, Christine Scott. Ms. Woeste worked as the project coordinator the second year. The completion of this research would have been much more difficult without her aid and assistance. Chriss is primarily responsible for the research and presentation of the data on the development of paraprofessionals in chapter 1. In addition, she spent numerous hours editing and proofreading the text.

Introduction

With public attention focused on high crime and recidivism rates, the field of corrections in recent years has been investigating alternative programs for crime prevention and control. One area receiving considerable attention has been the use of indigenous paraprofessionals.

Widespread use of indigenous workers within agencies began in 1963. The first major programs were funded under the President's Committee on Juvenile Delinquency and Youth Crime. The launching of the Office of Economic Opportunity in 1964 increased the need for the indigenous paraprofessional. Within a year, the OEO employed 25,000 paraprofessionals in community-action programs alone. Today, after new and modified legislation, the indigenous paraprofessional is a fact of life in the labor force. Not only have their numbers increased but their contributions and effectiveness have been repeatedly substantiated.

The indigenous paraprofessional is able to perform new and important services for social-service agencies. Because the indigenous paraprofessional has a background similar to the agency's clients, he is in an ideal position to assume a mediating role within the agency. The paraprofessionals can effectively interpret the agency to its clients as well as interpret the clients to the agency. In this manner not only are services more likely to be positively received, but the agency is more likely to adapt to its clients' needs. This is particularly true in the field of corrections, where the indigenous paraprofessionals are likely to be offenders or ex-offenders.

This volume reports on one attempt to use ex-offenders as paraprofessionals in the field of corrections. The State of Ohio, during the two-year period from 1972 through 1974, has successfully used ex-offenders in the parole department. The Parole Officer Aide Program was initiated by the Ohio Adult Parole Authority not only to gain the special services the ex-offenders can perform, but to provide new and meaningful careers for ex-offenders in the helping services. As the data analysis indicates, the program has been most effective in these and other areas.

In order to adequately understand the Parole Officer Aide Program, a brief history of the use of paraprofessionals in the helping services is reviewed. The Parole Officer Aide Program and the methodology used in evaluating it are then described. In addition, a thorough analysis is given of the program evaluation and its results. As part of the evaluation process, a national survey was conducted by the researchers to ascertain whether or not similar programs using ex-offenders are being considered or implemented by other correction departments. The findings of this survey are included in an effort to place the Ohio State Parole Officer Aide Program in perspective, with similar efforts being made in other states. Finally, the results and implications for future programs and directions in corrections are discussed.

1

Background and Development of the Use of Paraprofessionals

Recruiting nonprofessional aides for social-service programs is not a new idea. The most common type of aide is the volunteer, commonly used in such programs as the March of Dimes, the Red Cross, the League of Women Voters, etc. Most volunteers have no special qualifications for such programs, especially in the area of formal education; they are recruited for their desire to be of service to others, and because of their knowledge of community resources and opportunities. These nonprofessional volunteers are typically unpaid workers who provide regular and continuing services for the agency.[1] They are therefore viewed as distinct from the typical paid professional staff of an agency.

A modification of the volunteer program has been introduced into many human-service agencies. This new aid program incorporates the desirable attributes of the volunteer with the dimensions of a new career. The new worker, unlike his volunteer counterpart, is typically considered part of the agency's staff, and consequently is paid for his services, although he usually remains distinct from the formally trained professional. The name given to these new workers has gone through a number of changes since World War II. Titles such as "aide," "nonprofessional," "auxiliary," "paraprofessional," "subprofessional," "community worker," "new careerist," and "new professional" are but a few of the titles that have been used. According to Alan Gartner, these new titles are an attempt to attribute higher status to the workers who fill these positions.[2] Of these titles, "paraprofessional" is probably most commonly used by the human service agencies.

While paraprofessionals under various titles and roles were participating in New Deal programs as early as 1935, not until the 1960s did they gain much widespread popularity. The modern paraprofessionals made their first major debut in the school system, and quickly spread to health agencies and other social-service agencies. These first programs recruited largely middle-class persons to supplement the work of the trained professionals.

With the black, civil-rights, antiwar, and student movements of the sixties, a new awareness of human rights exploded on the American scene. A greater demand for more and for a better quality of life combined with a new element of community identification and community control met head on with the existing manpower resources. There were simply too few workers with the traditional social-biographical background and abilities to meet the new demand. Thus, a shift to a new type of manpower evolved—a man with definite community ties but less formal training. Reiff and Riessman saw this new

1

worker as "a peer of the client [who] shares a common background, language, ethnic origin, style and group of interests."[3] The indigenous paraprofessional, therefore, was born almost overnight.

The most obvious use of the indigenous paraprofessional is to increase service efficiency and effectiveness. This is done most frequently in two ways: by relieving the professional of time-consuming tasks that require little special training, and by providing new services not offered by the professional. It is within this second realm that the indigenous paraprofessional makes his special contribution to the service agency. The indigenous paraprofessional without formal training is capable of doing this because of his desire to be of service and his close community ties. These traits are especially helpful in dealing with minority and ethnic groups of which the professional may not be a member. Likewise, the indigenous paraprofessional is in an ideal position to influence the existing attitudes of the professionals concerning the members of the community, thus enabling the professional to deal more effectively with those he serves.

When most paraprofessionals were nonindigenous personnel, they were viewed as handmaidens of the professionals with whom they worked. There is a marked difference in the way in which indigenous personnel are viewed today. They are hired because of the unique contributions they can make to the local community and the agency in which they work. Research by Robert Carkhuff and others indicate that nonprofessionals can be as effective as trained professionals in dealing with certain problems and people.[4] Consequently, recent programs using indigenous workers have given these paraprofessionals major responsibilities in servicing client needs in the human services area.

Widespread use of indigenous workers within agencies and organizations began in 1963. The first major programs were funded under the President's Committee on Juvenile Delinquency and Youth Crime. MFY (Mobilization for Youth), located in New York City's Lower East Side, used indigenous persons in school and community work. This program led Frank Riessman to publish his first call for what he called "the new nonprofessional."[5]

In 1964, with the Economic Opportunity Act and the launching of the Office of Economic Opportunity (OEO), an increasing demand for the indigenous paraprofessional arose. The rash of new programs called for more and better services for the poor, and at the same time provided an opportunity for employment of these same people. After the first year, OEO employed 25,000 paraprofessionals in community-action programs and almost twice that number in the Head Start Program.[6]

By the late sixties, with new and modified legislation, indigenous paraprofessionals had become a fact of life in the labor force. Not only did their numbers increase, but their effectiveness was indisputable. Arthur Pearl and Frank Riessman have pinpointed the reasons for the paraprofessionals' success. They maintain that the paraprofessional, as a peer of those he served, became a "significant other" in the lives of his clients. Likewise, as a member being served by the community, the paraprofessional had "inside" knowledge about the workings of the community.[7]

It is little wonder with the success and development of the indigenous paraprofessional that the field of corrections latched onto the idea of using ex-offenders in various programs in corrections. The initial programs used offenders and ex-offenders as volunteers rather than paid paraprofessionals.

In 1964, two programs were begun within correctional facilities. The Draper Project, conducted at the Draper Correctional Center in Elmore, Alabama, was a unique approach to vocational and educational training. The project initiated a training program to be run solely by inmates, with many prisoners producing self-instructing educational materials.[8]

The Massachusetts Correctional Institution at Walpole developed a similar program, and the prisoners were encouraged to prepare instructional materials for their own use as well as for use by handicapped children and youth. The program, began under the direction of Dr. Harold Ruvin of the Department of Special Education of the Boston University School of Education, and is currently called "The New England Materials for Instruction Center."[9]

In March 1964, J.E. Baker, associate warden of the federal prison at Terre Haute, Indiana, reported on the use of inmate self-government programs throughout the United States in the *Journal of Criminal Law, Criminology, and Police Science.* Results of his study showed unsuccessful attempts at self-government at thirteen institutions. Baker noted that the major problem of such programs was their use of inmates as disciplinarians. Following his findings, Baker proposed the use of inmate advisory councils as a workable alternative, to permit inmates the opportunity to take a more active and constructive role in the improvement of the prison environment.[10]

The most characteristic element of these first programs of the sixties was the involvement of the inmate in self-help or self-improvement programs. Later programs moved a step further by using the offender and ex-offender in helping not only himself but others, especially members of his peer group.

Numerous other inmate counseling projects began in the sixties in several institutions such as the Colorado State Penitentiary (BARS Project), San Quentin (Squires' Program), and the Massachusetts Correctional Institution at Walpole (Project Youth). The focus in all of these programs is aimed at helping the youthful segment of the community, especially those singled out as potential offenders. Inmates meet with the juveniles and interested adults to share personal experiences and counsel potential delinquents about the disadvantages of antisocial behavior.[11]

In a somewhat different vein, the North Carolina Prison Department began a joint venture with the Institute of Government at the University of North Carolina, called the Chapel Hill Youth Development and Research Unit (CHYDARU). It was a camp for young felons transferred from the state penitentiary, and was staffed entirely by parolees.[12]

About the same time, Synanon Foundation began assisting a small prison camp on Peavine Mountain, north of Reno, Nevada. Three times a week the Synanon groups visited the prisoners to conduct discussion sessions or participate in recreational activities. Members of the Synanon group were themselves former inmates.[13]

In October 1969, the Norfolk Fellowship (a program bringing community members into the Massachusetts Correctional Institution at Norfolk to attend fellowship meetings with inmates) began Project Re-entry. The program allows ex-offenders who have "made it" on the outside to return to the prison and offer their experience and insights to men ready for release. After four and one-half years of experience, the program has proven to be quite successful, and the ex-offender is viewed by both prison officials and prisoners as a valuable resource.[14]

Since most of these correctional programs met with general success, an effort to extend the involvement of offenders and ex-offenders was initiated within the community setting. The Self-Development Group, Inc. is a program operating in Boston run by ex-convicts in which offenders, ex-offenders, and potential offenders attempt to aid one another in forming meaningful associations and curbing criminal behavior.[15]

The Seventh Step Program, begun at the Kansas state prison, is a prerelease program for inmates who are within four months of their release date. In 1965, the first facilities for helping released inmates began with the purpose of aiding convicted offenders to reestablish themselves in a community. Today the program extends from New York to California, aiding the ex-convict in finance, employment, housing, and friendship.[16]

The Future Association of Alberta, Canada and Efforts From Ex-Convicts (EFEC) in Washington, D.C., are both considered self-help programs run by ex-convicts with the purpose of aiding "ex-cons" in the process of reentry into the community. The Future Association offers a friendly atmosphere where previously incarcerated persons can meet people and make new friends who share common fears and problems.[17]

The House of Judah in Atlanta and Youth Development, Inc. are two community programs run by ex-convicts that attempt to provide service to youth in the area. The former focuses on juvenile runaways and drug users, and the latter addresses itself to teenagers exhibiting antisocial behavior.[18]

In the area of law enforcement, indigenous workers who have been involved in police-community-relations programs have met with great success. Of particular note is a program initiated by the Los Angeles Police in 1965 shortly after the Watts riots. The indigenous workers employed by the department were all school dropouts, and 75 percent were ex-offenders. They participated in community activities and aided police in crime and narcotic prevention.[19]

However, unlike the true paraprofessional programs, the initial programs in corrections cited above mostly offered voluntary or low-paying jobs for the offenders and ex-offenders. The major attribute lacking in such programs was continuing career possibilities in the helping field. Not until the development of the New Careers program in 1967 was the full potential of paraprofessionals in corrections realized. Rather than just providing supplementary helpers or volunteers, the New Careers program offered permanent jobs and a career-ladder concept to paraprofessionals. This new direction came about by an important amendment to the Economic Opportunity Act in 1966. The New Careers program probably did more than any other effort to insure the use of offenders as paraprofessionals in the field of corrections. It also changed the direction of using offenders as "correctional resources" to providing them with meaningful new careers. LaMar Empey pointed out the implications for corrections:

Our overriding concern is with new careers for offenders, not just with using offenders as a correctional resource. They are already being used as a resource. Our task now is to integrate that use into a larger scheme in which, by being of service to corrections, they might realize lasting career benefits.[20]

The field of corrections was ripe for the New Careers program. As Raymond D. Clements indicated in his handbook for parole officer aides, public attention has tended to focus on rising crime rates and punishment of the offender rather than on rehabilitation. Concomitantly, a critical problem exists in the administration of criminal justice in trying to adequately supervise and help offenders modify their behavior and conform to conventional standards. The social distance between the correction workers and the offenders has often been suggested as one of the major problems, resulting in recidivism and even higher crime rates.[21]

In 1968 the Joint Commission on Correctional Manpower and Training published a pamphlet that included several charts depicting employment of offenders and ex-offenders prior to this report.[22]

Table 1-1 indicates the employment of offenders and ex-offenders according to adult, juvenile, and combined adult and juvenile central offices. In all three offices, employment of offenders and ex-offenders did not approach the legally authorized number each agency could hire (e.g. three agencies were authorized to hire sixty-five such employees, while the survey indicated that only twenty-two offenders or ex-offenders were working in the three respective offices).

Tables 1-2 and 1-3 show the utilization of offenders and ex-offenders in specific activities at adult and juvenile institutions and at probation and parole agencies. Specified activities include teaching in academic or vocational programs, assisting in research projects, interviewing new inmates, and leading prerelease programs.

There is also a trend toward employing former inmates as regular staff members in standard correctional posts (as distinct from custodial or maintenance programs). Departments of Correction throughout the country are hiring ex-offenders as correctional officers, counselors, teachers, work-release

Table 1-1

Employment of Offenders and Ex-Offenders[a] in State Correctional Institutions, as Reported by State Central Offices for Institutions, 1967

Central Offices Reporting	Adult Central Offices		Combined Adult and Juvenile Central Offices		Juvenile Central Offices	
	Probationers and Parolees	Ex-Offenders	Probationers and Parolees	Ex-Offenders	Probationers and Parolees	Ex-Offenders
Restrictions on hiring:						
Legal restrictions	4	2	3	3	1	6
Policy restrictions	10	9	10	7	10	6
Ability to hire offenders	8	11	8	12	13	14
Employment of offenders and ex-offenders	7		9		6	

[a]Anyone who has been previously discharged, paroled, or placed on probation and is now free from legal supervision.

Source: Reports from 24 central offices for adult institutions only, 21 combined central offices for adult and juvenile institutions, and 26 central offices for juvenile institutions only, as of August 17, 1967.

Table 1-2
State Adult and Juvenile Institutions Utilizing Offenders and Ex-Offenders[a] in Specified Activities, 1967

	Juvenile Institutions Utilizing			Adult Institutions Utilizing		
	Inmates	Probationers and Parolees	Ex-Offenders	Inmates	Probationers and Parolees	Ex-Offenders
Teaching Academic or Vocational Programs	3	0	2	75	3	7
Leadership in Recreation Programs	28	0	3	75	2	1
Leadership in Rehabilitation Programs	12	1	3	32	8	10
Assistance in Research Projects	13	1	2	36	0	1
Interviewing New Inmates	8	0	0	29	0	1
Leadership in Prerelease Programs	11	1	3	13	12	12

[a]Anyone who has been previously discharged, paroled, or placed on probation and is now free from legal supervision.
Source: Reports from 227 adult institutions for the year preceding September 1, 1967; from 234 juvenile institutions for the year preceding March 1, 1967.

Table 1-3

State Probation and Parole Agencies Utilizing Offenders and Ex-Offenders[a] in Specified Activities, 1967

Activity	Probation and Parole Agencies Utilizing Probationers and Parolees	Ex-Offenders
Teaching or Leadership in Recreation Programs	0	1
Leadership in Rehabilitation Programs	5	4
Assistance in Research Projects	2	1
Interviewing New Probationers/Parolees	2	1
Leadership in Prerelease Programs	7	5
Clerical and Other Support Functions	2	3

[a]Anyone who has been previously discharged, paroled, or placed on probation and is now free from legal supervision.

Source: Reports from 7 state probation agencies, 49 state parole agencies, and 42 state parole and probation agencies combined, as of March 1, 1967.

placement officers, therapists in alcoholism and drug-addiction programs, and assistants to probation and parole officers.[23]

California is one of the states making extensive use of indigenous paraprofessionals in corrections. Project RODEO (Reduction of Delinquency through Expansion of Opportunity) is a good example of an overall effort to use ex-offenders to provide new services to the community. The professional and paraprofessional staff of RODEO supervise delinquent minors and those who ordinarily would be committed to institutions. The indigenous paraprofessionals were selected on the basis of their past community involvement and their ability to relate well in social settings. The director of the program, Ruth Rushen, feels that the indigenous workers not only are effective in handling their case loads but have been responsible for providing the trained professionals with new insights in dealing with problems of poverty and delinquency.[24]

Furthering this effort, California has begun the use of ex-offenders and indigenous workers as parole officer aides or assistants. California began the Parole Service Assistant Program in 1965, to provide job opportunities to hardcore unemployed and to improve the quality of parole services. Since then well over 300 paraprofessionals have worked in the department. By July 1968, parole aides had become liaisons between the parolee and the parole officer. They were expected and able to use their firsthand knowledge and experience in the community.[25]

Beginning in October 1968 and extending through September 1972, a two-phase program using paraprofessional probation officer assistants (POAs) was initiated and supervised by the University of Chicago's Center for Studies in Criminal Justice and the U.S. Probation Office, The Northern District of Illinois

(Chicago). A portion of these indigenous workers are ex-offenders. The POAs under the supervision of professionally trained probation officers provide direct services for probationers, and parolees. The study found the POAs to be judged effective by the professional probation officers.[26]

In 1971, Project MOST (Maximizing Oregon's Services and Training for Adult Probation and Parole) used three ex-offenders as paid staff members, functioning in the capacity of aides performing assignments at a paraprofessional level. They helped remove professional staff from routine, time-consuming activities. Project TEEM is an outgrowth of the pilot Project MOST in Oregon, and because of the success of the ex-offenders, continuation and expansion of the aide program was recommended.[27]

Conclusion

An overriding conclusion of programs using indigenous paraprofessionals has been their effectiveness. Not only does the community in which the indigenous paraprofessional work benefit from the services he provides, but as Frank Riessman and Arthur Pearl point out in *New Careers for the Poor*, the paraprofessional himself, as well as society, greatly benefits. The indigenous worker gains a new status by performing a meaningful job, by learning skills, and by helping others. Society as a whole benefits by providing better services to the poor, providing new jobs for the poor and minority group members, and filling manpower shortages in the area of social services despite widespread unemployment in the society as a whole.[28]

These phenomena are especially true in the case of the ex-offender paraprofessional. When ex-offenders are brought into programs, a sudden reversal of their roles takes place. The phenomenon "transforms recipients of help into dispensers of help."[29] Based on their experience with Synanon, Volkman and Cressey attribute the success of such programs to the role reversal of changing the reformee into the reformer.

The most effective mechanism for exerting group pressure on members will be found in groups so organized that criminals are induced to join with non-criminals for the purpose of changing other criminals. A group in which criminal A joins with some non-criminals to change criminal B is probably most effective in changing criminal A, not B. In order to change criminal B, criminal A must necessarily share the values of the anticriminal members.[30]

The trained professionals and the agencies in which the paraprofessional programs have developed have undergone considerable change as well. In his studies of Manpower projects, Grosser has provided evidence of the effect paraprofessionals have had on the professionals. The professionals learned new skills of interaction and new knowledge about the community. Grosser found that professionals in these projects are more effective with their clients than their counterparts in agencies without indigenous workers.[31] The agencies have often experienced a new social and political outlook as well. Likewise, a renewal effort toward accountability to the client and community has been precipitated.

In all areas it would appear that the introduction of the indigenous paraprofessional has been of great benefit to the clients, professionals, agencies, paraprofessionals themselves, and society as a whole. However, prior evaluations of programs using indigenous paraprofessionals in corrections have been primarily subjective and qualitative in nature. A real lack of empirical and objective data exists. It is necessary and essential for future investigations to provide the reliable and robust data that practitioners and theoreticians in corrections are demanding.

Summary

During the past decade indigenous workers with backgrounds or experience similar to those of the clients being served have been used by various agencies to establish closer, more productive relationships and to provide better services. The field of corrections has also begun using ex-offenders to achieve "role-reversal" effects and to aid present offenders in their rehabilitation and adjustment to the noninstitutional world.

The current trend is toward paid employment of indigenous individuals as regular staff members or as paraprofessionals. Of particular interest, California, Illinois, and Oregon have instituted programs employing ex-offenders as parole officer aides. While most of these efforts have been deemed successful, there remains a real lack of empirical research evaluating these programs.

2

The Parole Officer Aide Program in Ohio

With the growing popularity of using indigenous paraprofessionals in corrections, the State of Ohio investigated the feasibility of using ex-offenders as Parole Officer Aides (POAs). With the availability of federal funds, this program became a reality in 1972. This chapter discusses the inception, development, and implementation of the Parole Officer Aide Program in Ohio.

The Adult Parole Authority of the State of Ohio began the implementation of a program formally designated as the Parole Officer Aide Program in September 1972, to use ex-offenders as quasi-parole officers. This program is staffed solely by ex-offenders who have met the special requirements for admission to the program. Funding is provided by a grant from the Law Enforcement Assistance Administration and by matching state funds. The goals of the project are to bridge the gap between the Adult Parole Authority and parolees, to facilitate communication between corrections and the community, to engender trust and confidence in the correctional system, to decrease recidivism, and to reduce parole violations. During the first year, thirteen ex-offenders were hired as aides; an additional ten aides were employed the second year, bringing the total of ex-offender parole officer aides in Ohio to twenty-three. Approval was given to hire an additional six aides in 1974.

Salary

The ex-offenders working as parole officer aides do not enjoy the full status or salary of parole officers. The parole officer aide's position is classified as a Caseworker II under State Civil Service regulations, and the first-year parole officer is classified as a Parole Officer I. A Caseworker II's beginning salary is $3.70 per hour, for a yearly salary of $7696.00, while the Parole Officer I's beginning salary is $4.18 per hour or $8694.00 annually. Only one of the parole officer aides could be classified as a Parole Officer I, because the other aides lacked the educational requirement of at least three years of college. To complicate matters, the Caseworker II classification is next to the highest level possible in the Caseworker series, thus making promotions and/or salary increases (other than annual "step" raises) all but impossible at the present time. The Adult Parole Authority is working with the Ohio State Department of Personnel, however, to extend the Caseworker series so that the parole officer aides may achieve promotions to a salary range comparable to the parole

11

officer's. A proposal is also currently under consideration to allow aides to be promoted into the parole officer series. The Ohio Adult Parole Authority is taking a very progressive position in this regard, hoping to open the opportunity structure to the ex-offender aides. It appears very likely that a number of aides will be promoted to parole officer in the near future. This would set an important precedent and overcome many criticisms aimed at the new careers movement, specifically that indigenous workers are recruited into jobs that offer no future or hope for advancement. Based on the positive results of the ex-offender parole officer program in Ohio and the progressive leaders in Ohio's Adult Parole Authority, it is very likely that the career ladder for aides will shortly be a reality.

Duties of the Parole Officer Aide

The Ohio Parole Officer Aide Program differs from other parole aide programs now in operation throughout the country, in that each aide is assigned a caseload of thirty parolees and is required to provide "supervision comparable to supervision of professional officers."[1] The case load has been increased to fifty parolees for the 1974-75 fiscal year. The initial ten cases received by aides were drawn from the existing caseloads of parole officers within the same geographical unit as the one in which the aide worked. These ten cases were to be "multiple-problems" cases needing intensive supervision. The term "multiple problems" does not refer to the *severity* of a parolee's crime or life situation, but rather to the combination of social and/or behavioral problems impinging on the parolee. Parole regulations stipulated that all multiple-problems cases should consist only of men who would be "on the street," *not* awaiting arrest, trial, or further incarceration. The other twenty cases assigned to aides were theoretically to have been typical parolees. In reality, however, our evaluation indicates that the parole aides apparently receive parolees with more extensive criminal records, parolees incarcerated for longer periods of time, parolees whom other parole officers have often "given up on," and parolees about to be sent back to an institution.

The parole aides are also the key job resource developers for the Adult Parole Authority. It is generally felt that the aide is in a better position to locate employment possibilities for parolees than the parole officer because of the aide's intuitive understanding of the types of jobs parolees desire, as well as the aide's intimate knowledge of the neighborhoods in which the parolee is to work. These aptitudes of the parole aides are apparently providing a new expertise for the Adult Parole Authority previously not available. Our evaluation has substantiated the fact that parole officer aides are quite effective at job procurement for parolees.

Another important function of the aides is their ability to act as a resource for other staff members. Because the parole officer aides are generally familiar with high-delinquency neighborhoods within their working unit as well as the high-crime areas and establishments that should be avoided by parolees, their knowledge is invaluable to other parole officers in evaluating and counseling parolees. The parole aides are in an ideal position to share firsthand information about particular offenders and to suggest alternative supervision techniques.

An additional responsibility of the aides, as outlined in their job description, is that of speaking regularly before high schools, service groups, and prerelease institutional inmate groups to publicize the Adult Parole Authority's Programs and to gain the community support. As might be expected some aides have participated in this activity more extensively than others.

Limitations on the Parole Officer Aide

By law, the parole officer aide in Ohio is not allowed to: (1) arrest a parolee, (2) own or carry a firearm, or (3) transport an arrested offender. Also, due to statutory limitations, an aide cannot assume the responsibility of sole supervision over parolees. Thus, a weekly staffing of the aide's cases with the senior parole officer and unit supervisor is mandatory. (These are naturally carried out more judiciously by some unit supervisors than others, as will be apparent in the evaluation that follows.) In addition, monthly visits are theoretically required by the supervising officer to the home of parolees assigned to the parole officer aide to "collaborate information given at the weekly staffing, to determine attitudes of the offender and his family toward the aide, and to provide any additional assistance to the offender deemed necessary."

Selection and Assignment of Aides

The selection of the parole officer aides was initiated through recommendations by parole officers. The various districts of the Adult Parole Authority were informed of the program the first year and were asked to recommend qualified men who had successfully completed parole. Several ex-offenders were already involved in speaking engagements with parole officers or were volunteering for work around the office. These men showed an interest in the work of the parole department, and some were considered "naturals" for the job. Men were also recruited from successful community programs using ex-offenders, such as Seven Steps and Con-cerns. Recommendations were forwarded to the Project Director who, along with top administrators of the Adult Parole Authority, selected thirteen men to begin in August 1972. The additional aides hired in 1973 were selected in a somewhat different manner. Parole units in which new aides were to work selected prospects who were then approved by the Central Office.

The following selection criteria for parole officer aides were established and (generally) followed:

1. Age—there was a reluctance to hire men younger than twenty-two.
2. Residency—all applicants were required to be Ohio residents.
3. Parole status—all applicants had to have successfully completed parole.
4. Communication skills—applicants had to demonstrate a propensity for interpersonal communication skills (be articulate), and be free of psychopathological tendencies.
5. Applicants must have displayed "acceptable" behavior during incarceration.
6. Applicants must have displayed sufficient "coping" ability and genuine concern for others.
7. Applicants' behavior must not have been considered excessively assaultive, or aggressive, to the point of being dysfunctional.

To facilitate a successful beginning, the project director was careful to select "winners"—men he was confident would succeed. Of the thirteen men chosen in August 1972, ten remained as active and successful parole officer aides as of August 1974. One man resigned after discovering he was not suited for the program, one was dismissed because of an alcohol problem, and one was promoted to the Ohio Department of Rehabilitation and Corrections as an ombudsman. The additional aides hired in 1973 have not been quite so successful in maintaining employment. One was dismissed because of suspicious and possibly criminal activity; another was dismissed because of his presence at an illegal house of gambling; a third quit because of his dissatisfaction with the restriction prohibiting his carrying a firearm; and a fourth was promoted to the state ombudsman's office (the second aide to be promoted to that office). The aides who resigned or were dismissed have all been replaced by other offenders. Tentative plans call for the utilization of twenty-nine aides during the 1974-75 year, necessitating the recruitment and hiring of an additional six aides.

Description of Ohio's Parole Officer Aides

The twenty-three aides employed by the Ohio Adult Parole Authority as of June 1974 come from diverse backgrounds. Although most come from blue-collar backgrounds, their previous occupations range from sheriff's deputy, undercover agent, employment placement specialist, welder, roofer, landscaper, and salesman, to more menial jobs such as custodian, porter, cab driver, grave digger, and gas-station attendant. The aides' formal education is considerably less than the average parole officer's. Only one has a college degree, and nine have not completed high school.

The aides' past criminal involvement varies considerably as well. The number of arrests for aides varies from 1 to 21 with an average of 6.2. The number of convictions also varies considerably, from 1 to 21, with an average of 4.2. The actual time aides had previously been incarcerated ranges from 11 months to 10 years, the average time being 51.3 months per aide. The offenses for which they had been incarcerated ranged from murder, manslaughter, robbery, and assault and battery to passing bad checks, auto theft, burglary, receiving stolen goods, and carrying a concealed weapon. Judging from the above data, the parole officer aides hired by the Ohio Adult Parole Authority are certainly experienced in the field of crime.

Training Seminar

Prior to entering the field on a full-time basis, all of the first-year parole officer aides were involved in a two-week training seminar along with their future supervisors. The agenda for the first week included several speakers from the Adult Parole Authority, who discussed the philosophy, goals, and objectives of the program; the various roles of the parole officer aide; counseling and interviewing techniques; the criminal justice system; the use of community resources; and parole philosophy as it relates to the community. The seminar also included instructions on report writing and the proper procedures for completing departmental forms.

During the second week, sessions were conducted by Program Design and Implementation, a subsidiary of Executive General Corporation. Various models of communication were discussed, as well as team building and practical planning. Individual speakers discussed psychological hang-ups and psychological "bigness." The Leadership Planning Guide from Management Research Associates was used to evaluate all participants in the seminar. This information was also helpful in breaking down initial barriers between the aides and their supervisors and promoting communication crucial to the program's success.

The subsequent training seminar for the second group of parole officer aides was conducted by Public Service Careers, Inc., and lasted four weeks. The format for this second seminar covered essentially the same areas as the first; however, additional emphasis was given to verbal, writing, and counseling skills.

Evaluation

In September 1972, the Adult Parole Authority contracted with the Program for the Study of Crime and Delinquency of the Ohio State University to conduct an evaluative study of the Parole Officer Aide Project. The following information in this volume concerns that evaluation, and will be covered in detail in Chapters 3, 4, 5, and 6.

Summary

Since September 1972, Ohio has employed ex-offenders to work as parole officer aides. Selected on the basis of successful parole completion, past behavior and personal capabilities, the parole officer aides have performed tasks similar to those of a parole officer. Specifically, the parole officer aide is responsible for a caseload of thirty parolees, performs some public-relations activities, and serves as a resource for other staff members. Men selected as parole officer aides received intensive training concerning the Adult Parole Authority goals, and objectives as well as training concerning more mundane and parochial matters.

3

Methodology

In this chapter the methodology used in evaluating Ohio's Parole Officer Aide Program is discussed. The first part of the chapter briefly describes the goals of the evaluation and the various means utilized in attempting to reach these goals, and the second part consists of a more extensive description and explanation of the various approaches utilized in evaluating the program, as well as identifying for the reader the specific indices and scales utilized by the researchers. In addition, several limitations of this evaluation and report are noted, and some suggestions are made for future evaluations. The results and analysis of the data will be reserved for subsequent chapters.

Goals of the Evaluation

The primary goal in evaluating the Parole Officer Aide Program was to determine the effectiveness of ex-offenders working as parole officer aides for the Adult Parole Authority. Inasmuch as the ex-offenders (parole officer aides) were not *necessarily* going to be performing tasks identical to those of traditional parole officers, utilizing some type of quasi-experimental design was not feasible. The decision was made to use a compromise research design (i.e., comparing aides to parole officers on those tasks that both groups would be performing).

Certainly one of the major limitations of the Parole Officer Aide Program evaluation is the lack of any equivalent group with which to compare results. For evaluators to conclude on the basis of their data analysis that a program is effective and worthwhile, or ineffective and worthless, it must be in relation to something else. This was the reason a control group was selected. Each parole officer selected as a member of the control group worked in one of the geographical units to which an aide was assigned, and was also the officer in that unit most like the aide with respect to prior work experience with the Adult Parole Authority (i.e., generally, the youngest parole officer in terms of work experience). Using such a control group allowed us to reach certain general conclusions that we otherwise would not have.

As was indicated in Chapter 2, aides not only had fewer cases than parole officers, but had a higher percentage of multiple-problems cases. (Generally one-third of the aide's caseload was made up of parolees with multiple problems.) In addition, aides were sometimes assigned other officers' parolees who had repeatedly broken rules and were in danger of having their parole

17

18

revoked. Given the different nature of the aide's caseload and the typical parole officer's caseload, comparisons on such normal indicators as parolees' recidivism rates might therefore be very misleading.

Approaches Utilized in Evaluating the Program

The Parole Officer Aide Program has been continuously monitored and evaluated since the program's inception in September 1972. Several approaches have been used. *First*, a questionnaire was developed to measure various attitudes and orientations generally associated with effective social service personnel. This questionnaire was administered each year (once in 1972 and again in 1973) to all parole officer aides and all parole officers in Ohio. *Second*, after the Parole Officer Aide Program was essentially under way, in-depth interviews were conducted by a professional interviewer with each of the parole officer aides. The primary purpose of these interviews was to discover any problems aides might be having with their new responsibilities, as well as to determine their effectiveness. *Third*, undergraduate students (primarily juniors and seniors) from Ohio State University worked an entire day with either a parole officer aide or a parole officer. (Ten parole officers were selected as a control group the first year, and twenty-three the second.) These students, trained as participant observers and instructed on field procedures and recording of information for later analysis, reported the activities and evaluated the effectiveness of the parole officers and aides with whom they worked. *Fourth*, each unit supervisor was interviewed both years and asked to rate the effectiveness of parole officer aides and the parole officers in the control group under his jurisdiction. *Fifth*, inmates at Ohio's adult penal institutions, who were at the time participating in a prerelease program, were administered questionnaires to poll their attitudes concerning the appropriateness of the aide program. *Sixth*, a fairly large sample of the parolees supervised by parole officer aides or the parole officers in the control group were surveyed concerning their attitudes and evaluations of the services rendered by the officer or aide who directly supervised them. These parolees were mailed a questionnaire on which they rated the quality and quantity of supervision they received. Additional information about the parolees polled was obtained from the Adult Parole Authority files for comparative purposes. *Seventh*, the second year's evaluation also included a national survey of State Directors of Correction, to determine the prevalence and desirability of ex-offender programs in corrections.

Attitudinal Questionnaire

One of the first tasks the evaluators undertook was the construction and administration of a tool designed to measure respondents' attitudes and orientations toward working with and relating to people. Essentially the same instrument was administered both years. This instrument was administered to all parole officers and aides at their respective district meetings.

The questionnaires were administered to 102 men the first year, 89 of whom were parole officers and 13 parole officer aides. The second year 126 employees, of whom 19 were parole officer aides, completed the questionnaire.

In looking at the social characteristics of the two groups (see Table 3-1), certain demographic differences are apparent. (The reader may note that on a number of the questions for the first year, certain demographic information is missing on a large number of parole officers. The reason for this lacuna is simply that those questions were added to the questionnaire after it had already been administered to a large number of the parole officers.) The aides are composed of a much greater percentage of blacks than are the parole officers (54 percent compared to 24 percent in 1973, and 63 percent compared to 18 percent in 1974). The men working as aides also had considerably less formal schooling than did the parole officers. The majority of the aides had not finished high school, while the majority of the parole officers were college graduates. Also, a higher percentage of parole officers than parole aides were married (92 percent compared to 62 percent in 1973 and 66 percent compared to 58 percent in 1974).

Several scales were included in this initial questionnaire. An achievement motivation scale was used, composed of the following ten items:

1. I like to do my very best in whatever I undertake.
2. I would like to do something that means a lot to other people.
3. If somebody says I'm not good enough, I usually try harder.
4. I like to succeed in the things that I do.
5. The easier the job, the better I like it.
6. I try to be better at things than most people.
7. Doing hard jobs makes me proud.
8. I don't like people who are always trying to get ahead.
9. I would like to accomplish something of great significance.
10. I like the challenge of a hard job.[1]

A self-esteem scale composed of ten questions was included:

1. Once people get to know me they usually don't like me.
2. I don't have too much respect for myself.
3. I think that most people like me.
4. I will never amount to anything worthwhile.
5. The more people know about me, the less they like me.
6. I don't believe that anyone really likes me.
7. I'm not much good for anything.
8. There's nothing about me that is any good.

Table 3-1

Social Characteristics of the Respondents to the Attitudinal Questionnaire[a]

| | 1973 Respondents | | | | 1974 Respondents | | | |
| | Parole Aides | | Parole Officers | | Parole Aides | | Parole Officers | |
	Number	%	Number	%	Number	%	Number	%
Sex								
Male	13	100.0	85	95.5	18	94.7	102	95.3
Female	0	0.0	4	4.5	1	5.3	5	4.7
Race								
White	6	46.2	68	76.4	7	36.8	87	82.1
Black	7	53.8	21	23.6	12	63.2	19	17.9
Age								
22-25	2	15.4	18	21.7	1	5.3	32	31.1
26-31	2	15.4	24	28.9	5	26.3	38	36.9
32-44	8	61.5	20	24.1	11	57.9	19	18.4
45-67	1	7.7	21	25.3	2	10.5	14	13.6
Marital Status								
Married	8	61.5	12	92.3	11	55.0	69	65.7
Divorced or separated	1	7.7	0	0.0	3	15.0	7	6.7
Single	4	30.8	1	7.7	6	30.0	29	27.6

	N	%	N	%	N	%	N	%
Education								
Less than high school	7	53.8	0	0.0	7	36.8	0	0.0
High-school graduate	2	15.4	2	2.3	5	26.3	5	4.7
2 years or less of college	2	15.4	2	2.3	4	21.1	1	0.9
More than 2 years of college	1	7.7	7	8.0	2	10.5	4	3.8
College degree	1	7.7	53	60.9	1	5.3	57	53.8
Graduate studies	0	0.0	23	26.4	0	0.0	39	36.8
Father's Occupation								
Unskilled employee	2	20.0	1	7.7	4	21.1	15	14.4
Semi-skilled employee	3	30.0	2	15.4	7	36.8	13	12.5
Skilled manual employee	5	50.0	4	30.8	3	15.8	34	32.7
Clerical & sales worker	0	0.0	1	7.7	0	0.0	4	3.8
Administrative personnel (owner of small business, minor professionals)	0	0.0	4	30.8	2	10.5	23	22.1
Business managers	0	0.0	0	0.0	2	10.5	4	3.8
Higher executives	0	0.0	1	7.7	1	5.3	11	10.6
Length of Parole Service								
Less than 1 year	13	100.0	16	18.4	9	47.4	26	24.3
1-2 years	0	0.0	21	24.1	10	52.6	36	33.6
3 years or more	0	0.0	50	57.5	0	0.0	45	42.1

aPercentages in this and subsequent tables may not add to 100 percent due to rounding error. The N may also differ due to missing data.

9. Sometimes, I think I'm no good at all.

10. All in all, I would say that I am a failure.[2]

A focal concerns scale which included ten statements was employed:

1. I'd rather not have anyone telling me what to do.

2. Never back down from a fight.

3. You shouldn't waste your time on anything that is not exciting.

4. Excitement makes life worth living.

5. You can get what you want from other people if you can outsmart them.

6. The most successful men got that way by being lucky.

7. You've got to be able to fight your way out of tough spots.

8. The only thing I have to look foward to is whatever excitement I can find.

9. Anything that is not exciting is not worth doing.

10. The tough guy has it made.

A parole aide scale consisting of thirty-six separate indicators was also developed and utilized:

1. The parole officer aide (POA) can be a valuable assistant to the parole officer.

2. The POA's prior criminal status will lessen his ability to line up jobs for parolees.

3. POAs have a unique understanding of problems of present parolees.

4. There are few qualified POAs who can do effective parole work.

5. POAs will be as effective in changing present parolees as are parole officers.

6. POAs will undermine the parole officer's position with parolees.

7. The best agent for changing parolees is the POA.

8. Most parolees will see POAs as a stool pigeon for the correctional system.

9. Use of POAs will improve the agency's public image.

10. POAs will demand too much time and effort in supervision by parole officers.

11. The use of POAs will probably result in new treatment programs that will help parolees adjust to the street.

12. POAs will be torn between loyalty to the parolee and to the correctional agency.

13. Using POAs is highly likely to reduce parole violations in their case loads.

14. POAs have little to offer the criminal justice system.

15. In general, POAs are able to carry the same caseload as a parole officer.

16. POAs would be more effective with multiple problems cases than with a general caseload.

17. Most POAs will have problems relating to the average parole case.
18. As far as the acceptance of other ex-offenders by the community is concerned, the use of POAs is likely to be useful to corrections.
19. POAs would be more effective in institutional work rather than parole work.
20. The POA will affect the image of the parole officer positively.
21. Most parolees would object to being supervised by a POA rather than a parole officer.
22. POAs decrease the gap between parolees and the parole system.
23. The POA will affect the image of the parole officer positively.
24. POAs are able to promote positive public relations for the parole system.
25. Using POAs will not increase trust of parolees in the parole system.
26. Parolees who are assisted by POAs are more likely to succeed on parole than those who do not receive such help.
27. POAs will not be as effective as the parole officer since the parolee will not see him as an authority figure.
28. POAs can establish productive relations with non-middle class parolees which parole officers would find most difficult to establish.
29. Most POAs tend to overlook technical violations of parolees.
30. It is easy for a POA to help parolees avoid pitfalls which he has already made.
31. Most POAs will not be as dedicated to changing parolees as will parole officers.
32. Using POAs will increase trust of parolees in the parole system.
33. POAs are as effective in changing behavior of parolees as are parole officers.
34. Parole officers are more effective in changing behavior of parolees than are POAs.
35. The use of POAs can reduce recidivism among parolees.
36. POAs can supervise parolees with a minimum of difficulty.

Srole's anomia scale was also utilized, consisting of five statements:

1. Most public officials (people in public office) are not really interested in the problems of the average man. In general, would you agree with that statement or disagree?
2. These days a person doesn't really know whom he can count on.
3. Nowadays, a person has to live pretty much for today and let tomorrow take care of itself.
4. In spite of what some people say, the lot (condition) of the average man is getting worse, not better.
5. It's hardly fair to bring a child into the world with the way things look for the future.[3]

A powerlessness scale composed of seven questions was used:

1. There's very little we can do to keep prices from going higher.
2. Persons like myself have little chance of protecting their personal interests when they conflict with those of strong pressure groups.
3. A lasting world peace can be achieved by those of us who work toward it.
4. I think each of us can do a great deal to improve world opinion of the United States.
5. This world is run by the few people in power, and there is not much the little guy can do about it.
6. People like me can change the course of world events if we make ourselves heard.
7. More and more, I feel helpless in the face of what's happening in the world today.[4]

A conservatism scale made up of nine questions was included:

1. If you start trying to change things very much, you usually make them worse.
2. No matter how we like to talk about it, political authority really comes not from us, but from some higher power.
3. It's better to stick by what you have than to be trying new things you don't really know about.
4. A man doesn't really get to have much wisdom until he's well along in years.
5. I prefer the *practical* man any time to the man of ideas.
6. If something grows up over a long time, there will always be much wisdom in it.
7. I'd want to know that something would really work before I'd be willing to take a chance on it.
8. All groups can live in harmony in this country without changing the system in any way.
9. We must respect the work of our forefathers and not think that we know better than they did.[5]

Two dogmatism scales were incorporated into the questionnaire. One of them[6] consisted of all fifteen items listed below, while the other scale[7] included only the first ten:

1. Fundamentally, the world we live in is a pretty lonely place.
2. It is often desirable to reserve judgment about what's going on.
3. A person who thinks primarily of his own happiness is beneath contempt.
4. In the history of mankind there have probably been just a handful of really great thinkers.

5. Most people just don't know what's good for them.

6. Once I get wound up in a heated discussion I just can't stop.

7. The worst crime a person can commit is to attack publicly the people who believe in the same thing he does.

8. In this complicated world of ours the only way we know what is going on is to rely upon leaders or experts who can be trusted.

9. In the long run the best way to live is to pick friends and associates whose tastes and beliefs are the same as one's own.

10. While I don't like to admit this even to myself, I sometimes have the ambition to become a great man like Einstein, Beethoven, or Shakespeare.

11. My blood boils whenever a person stubbornly refuses to admit he's wrong.

12. There are two kinds of people in this world: those who are for the truth and those who are against the truth.

13. Man on his own is a helpless and miserable creature.

14. It is better to be a dead hero than to be a live coward.

15. The present is all too often full of unhappiness. It is only the future that counts.

In addition to the attitudinal scales and indices, and the social biographical data, the questionnaire focused on the orientations concerning corrections and, more specifically, the causes of crime, as viewed by the aides and officers.

In-depth Interviews of Parole Officer Aides

In-depth interviews were conducted during the first evaluation year with each parole officer aide. A professional interviewer was hired to travel to the various Ohio cities in which aides were working. On-the-job interviews were conducted in Akron, Athens, Canton, Cincinnati, Cleveland, Columbus, Dayton, Lima, Toledo, and Youngstown. The major focus of this portion of the evaluation was to ascertain how well the aides had been assimilated into the Adult Parole Authority, how well they were functioning, and if any major problems were being encountered. A copy of the questionnaire used by the interviewer is included in the appendix. In addition, several questions were asked as to how aides utilized their work time and how satisfied they were with their work.

Field Observations of Officers and Aides

As part of the evaluation, information was desired on the relationship between parole officer aides and the parolees they supervised, as compared to traditional parole officers. Of interest as well was the way in which aides compared to parole officers utilized their working hours.

At this point in the evaluation it was determined that some type of control group was needed for comparative purposes. This group would serve as a reference point for the parole officer aides. Although a parole officer aide's job description differed somewhat from a parole officer's, the similarities between the two appear to be greater than the differences.

The first control group was selected in March 1973. At that time, only ten of the original thirteen aides were still employed by the Adult Parole Authority. Ten parole officers were therefore selected in the manner described above. These ten officers are the control group for the 1973 evaluation, and many of the comparisons will be in reference to their behavior and job performance. A similar procedure was followed the second year, when twenty-three parole officers were selected as the control group. From this point on, when reference is made to parole officers, it will denote those men comprising the control group, unless otherwise specified.

It was originally planned for unit supervisors to rate both aides and parole officers on their ability to relate with parolees, as well as to have a sample of parolees rate each group on various criteria. In addition, it was felt that valid insights might be gained by having someone work with members of each group and keep reliable records on a number of items.

Nineteen junior and senior students from The Ohio State University were selected for this part of the data collection the first year, and forty-six the second year. They received instructions on methods of participant observation and various ways to collect data in an unobtrusive and nonreactive manner. Each student was also provided with a brief outline of questions he was to answer following his field work. Two or three days following each student's field work, one of the research staff members at the Center for the Study of Crime and Delinquency met with the students individually for a "debriefing" interview. These interviews generally took about thirty minutes to complete. The student's written report was gone over at this time, and other information that will be discussed in Chapter 4 was solicited from each student.

The research staff was aware of the possibility of selective perception and retention of information on the part of the field participants. It was felt, however, that any biasing of such perceptions would be randomly distributed between the two groups (parole officer aides and parole officers), inasmuch as no effort was made to match type of field worker with type of Adult Parole Authority employee. As a precaution, however, students were simply informed that they would be working with a parole officer, and that the purpose of our evaluation was to provide the Adult Parole Authority with an indication of a typical day for a parole officer in Ohio. No mention was made of the fact that some of the parole officers were former offenders. Similarly, parole officers and aides were simply requested to allow a student registered in the author's criminology course at Ohio State University to work with them for a day to see what parole officers do.

Field workers recorded specific information on the following topics:

1. Number of parolees seen during the day;
2. What percentage of the officers' time was spent with parolees;
3. How well the officer got along with parolees and with fellow staff members.

A copy of the outline for each student's written report is included in the appendix.

Interviews with Unit Supervisors

Each unit supervisor in whose unit a parole officer aide worked was interviewed in late March 1973, and again in March 1974, by one of the research staff members from the Crime and Delinquency Center. The number of unit supervisors increased from ten to twenty during the second year's study. The supervisors were asked to evaluate the aide working in their unit as well as the parole officer (selected as a member of the control group) on several characteristics.

The questions used for these interviews were developed from discussions with several staff members of the Adult Parole Authority. Three characteristics repeatedly mentioned as necessary for a parole officer to perform well on his job were used in measuring the effectiveness of officers and aides from their supervisor's perspective:

1. The officer's ability to motivate parolees;
2. The officer's ability to relate in a nonthreatening and yet firm manner to parolees;
3. The officer's willingness to put himself out, or in other words "go the extra mile" in working with parolees.

The supervisor was asked to rate the aide and the "control" parole officer on each of the above characteristics, using a scale from zero to one hundred. The scale was presented in the following manner:

Poor					Average					Excellent
0	10	20	30	40	50	60	70	80	90	100

Using this same type of rating scale, supervisors were asked to indicate how the aide or officer under his supervision ranked with respect to: (1) getting jobs or special job training for parolees; (2) getting along with fellow workers; (3) getting along with representatives of other programs and agencies in the community; (4) report writing; and (5) as an overall employee of the Adult Parole

Authority. Data was also gathered from supervisors at this time on the advantages and disadvantages of the Parole Officer Aide Program, and on any additional activities in which aides had been engaged that were not generally performed by parole officers.

Inmates' Attitudes Toward the
Parole Officer Aide Program

The fifth method utilized in evaluating the Parole Officer Aide Program was to have inmates who were about to be released from prison rate the advantages and disadvantages of such an approach. Inasmuch as all parole officers' and aides' ultimate job is to help inmates released from penal institutions adjust to and function adequately in society, it seemed logical to ascertain what these past offenders felt about the use of ex-offenders in corrections.

The research design originally called for the administration of a question-naire, in April 1973, to inmates in the prerelease program of all penal institutions for felony offenders in Ohio. Because of budgetary and time limitations, this questionnaire was administered only to those inmates in the prerelease program at the two male institutions at Lebanon and Mansfield. However, during the second year's evaluation, inmates in the prerelease programs from all penal institutions in Ohio were included in the sample. The number of inmates (65) responding to the questionnaire the first year is therefore somewhat limited. A more adequate sample size was obtained the second year, with 180 respondents. Table 3-2 reveals several characteristics of these two samples.

The second year's sample contained a larger percentage of blacks (52 percent in 1974 as compared to 44 percent in 1973), a wider age distribution, and a larger percentage of high-school graduates (39 percent in 1974 as compared to 14 percent in 1973). These changes appear to reflect changes in the inmate composition of Ohio's prisons. For example, in 1973 less than 50 percent of the inmates were black; in May of 1974, the Adult Parole Authority reported that 58 percent of the inmates were black.

Survey of Parolees

The sixth approach used in evaluating the aide program was a survey of the parolees supervised by aides and "control" officers. It was felt that the parolees could indicate the effectiveness of aides in comparison to parole officers as well as or better than any other group.

A sample of twenty parolees the first year and ten parolees the following year was randomly selected from each officer's and aide's caseload. Inasmuch as the

Table 3-2

Social and Demographic Characteristics of Inmates from Ohio Correctional Institutions Responding to Questions Concerning the Parole Officer Aide Program

	1973 Respondents		1974 Respondents	
	Number	Percentage	Number	Percentage
1. What is your race?				
Black	28	43.7	90	51.7
White	36	56.3	81	46.5
Other	0	0	3	1.8
2. On your last birthday, how old were you?				
18-21	22	36.6	18	10.4
22-25	30	50.0	38	22.0
26-30	8	13.4	38	22.0
Over 30	0	0	79	45.6
3. How many years of school have you completed?				
0-3 years	0	0	3	1.7
4-6 years	0	0	5	2.9
7-8 years	10	15.6	21	12.1
9-11 years (some high school or trade school)	37	57.8	67	38.7
12 years (high-school graduate)	9	14.0	57	32.9
13-15 years (some college or technical school)	8	12.5	18	10.4
16 years or more (college graduate)	0	0	2	1.1
4. How many times in your life have you been arrested?				
1-2	6	16.2	52	28.9
3-5	12	32.4	49	27.2
6-10	7	18.9	30	16.7
11-20	6	16.2	16	8.9
More than 20	1	2.7	7	3.9
Unspecified	5	13.5	26	14.4
5. How old were you when you were first arrested?				
Under 10	5	13.5	5	2.9
10-15	16	43.2	48	28.2

Table 3-2 (cont.)

	1973 Respondents		1974 Respondents	
	Number	Percentage	Number	Percentage
16-18	8	21.6	50	29.4
19-21	6	16.2	22	12.9
22-25	2	5.4	16	9.4
Over 25	0	0	29	17.0

(Median age at first arrest:
1973 = 14; 1974 = 18)

(Mean age at first arrest:
1973 = 15 yr. 1 1/2 mo.;
1974 = 20 yr. 1.9 mo.)

6. How much time have you spent altogether in correctional institutions?

	1973 Respondents		1974 Respondents	
	Number	Percentage	Number	Percentage
Less than 1 year	0	0	1	.5
More than 1 year but less than 3 years	20	54.1	48	28.6
More than 3 years but less than 7 years	12	32.4	66	39.3
7 years or more	5	13.5	53	31.5

(Mean time incarcerated:
1973 = 45 mo.;
1974 = 67.2 mo.)

7. Have you ever been on parole?

	1973 Respondents		1974 Respondents	
	Number	Percentage	Number	Percentage
Yes	16	40.0	78	43.8
No	24	60.0	100	56.2

caseloads of many parole officer aides differed significantly from those of other parole officers, each unit supervisor was requested to go over the list of parolees on the "control" officer's caseload and select the thirty parolees most similar to those he would assign the aide. From these thirty names each year, a sample of parolees was randomly selected. This approach seemed necessary to us in order to have somewhat similar groups of parolees to evaluate the aides and the officers because of possible differences in type of parolees on various caseloads. As previously indicated, some unit supervisors had voiced apprehension about assigning potentially violent parolees to aides, while other supervisors indicated they assigned the "worst" parolees in their unit to the aide.

This type of research design was again a compromise from the original approach. At the beginning of the aide program, twenty of the thirty parolees whom the aides were to supervise were to be randomly assigned from a list of new parolees being released from the penal institutions. (The other ten cases had already been assigned and were "multiple problems" in nature.) Parolees were to be assigned to aides whose parole unit corresponded to the geographical location of the parolee's residence. Some unit supervisors flatly refused to assign certain types of parolees to an aide; thus, the caseload that an aide received varied accordingly.

The compiling of the sample of 400 parolees' names and addresses the first year and 460 the second took some time, and required a substantial effort on the part of the research staff. More than five letters were sent to some unit supervisors, and numerous long-distance telephone calls were made, before a list of thirty parolees' names and addresses was acquired.

The first year personalized letters explaining very simply the nature of the evaluation and asking for help were individually typed and sent to each parolee. The second year form letters were used. These letters, along with a printed questionnaire and a preaddressed, stamped return envelope were sent by air mail to each parolee. Five days later the first follow-up letter was mailed to parolees who had not responded, reminding them to return the questionnaire. The second follow-up letter was sent approximately ten days after the original mailing. A fourth letter, along with another copy of the questionnaire, was mailed to nonrespondents two weeks following the original mailing. A fifth letter was also sent requesting the parolees' help in the study. (A sample copy of the letters and the questionnaire used are in the appendix.)

Although the total sample size was to be 400 parolees the first year and 460 the second, several parolees had either been reincarcerated or had their parole terminated before our first mailing. In addition, the mailed materials could not be delivered to several parolees because of incorrect addresses and no forwarding addresses. These factors reduced the potential respondents to 357 parolees the first year and 418 the second. The composition of the original sample, those contacted, and those who completed and returned the questionnaire is presented in Table 3-3.

The social characteristics of the parolees returning the questionnaire are recorded in Table 3-4, according to whether they were under the supervision of an aide or a parole officer. On the average, the parolees supervised by aides appear to be somewhat older than those under the supervision of parole officers (32.2 years compared with 29.9 years in 1973, and 31.3 years versus 31.2 years in 1974). The aides' caseloads also consist of a much higher percentage of blacks than do the parole officers' caseloads (67.6 percent compared with 30.1 percent in 1973, and 63.5 percent compared with 52.2 percent in 1974). On the average, parolees under the supervision of aides have completed fewer years of formal schooling than parolees being supervised by parole officers, and parolees supervised by aides in 1974 earned on the average considerably less money per week than parole officers' parolees. Parolees under the supervision of aides also had more extensive criminal records,[8] and experienced their first arrest on the average a year and a half earlier than parolees supervised by parole officers.

Table 3-3
Information on Sample of Parolees Surveyed

	Parolees Supervised by 1973 Respondents			Parolees Supervised by 1974 Respondents		
	Parole Officer Aides	Parole Officers	Total	Parole Officer Aides	Parole Officers	Total
Original sample	200	200	400	230	230	460
Lost due to reincarceration or termination of parole	5	1	6	8	3	11
Lost due to wrong address or no forwarding address	18	19	37	17	14	31
Sample contacted	177	180	357	205	213	418
Questionnaires returned	105	103	208	126	140	266
Percentage of contacted sample returning questionnaires	59.3%	57.2%	58.3%	61.2%	65.7%	63.6%

Table 3-4
Social Characteristics of Respondents to the Survey of Parolees According to Whether Supervised by a Parole Officer Aide or a Parole Officer

| | 1973 Respondents | | | | 1974 Respondents | | | |
| | Parole Aides | | Parole Officers | | Parole Aides | | Parole Officers | |
	N	%	N	%	N	%	N	%
Age (average)	103	32.2	105	29.9	126	31.3	140	31.2
Race								
White	32	30.5	71	68.9	46	36.5	66	47.8
Black	71	67.6	31	30.1	80	63.5	72	52.2
Education								
8 years or less	32	30.5	25	24.3	25	19.8	23	16.4
9-11 years	51	48.6	38	36.9	63	50.0	61	43.6
12 years or more	22	21.0	40	38.8	38	30.2	56	40.0
Income (average per week)								
Unemployed or none	15	14.3	20	19.4	22	20.2	25	20.0
$75 or less	25	23.8	21	20.4	26	23.9	18	14.4
$76-$125	40	38.1	39	37.9	30	27.5	38	30.4
$126 or more	25	23.8	23	22.3	31	28.4	44	35.2
Average length of incarceration for most recent offense (months)	103	37.0	96	33.7	126	31.2	140	31.0
Prior criminal involvement score	–	–	–	–	126	228	140	192
Age at first arrest	–	–	–	–	126	17.8	140	19.3

Even with the use of a somewhat similar control group, the evaluation of aides' performance was still somewhat limited by the fact that the caseload of aides and parole officers differed both with respect to size and possibly "types" of parolees. Nevertheless, many valid and reliable conclusions can be drawn from the evaluation.

Survey of the Fifty States

For the second year's evaluation, data was gathered on similar programs employing ex-offenders throughout the United States. With this as the goal, a survey questionnaire was mailed to administrative heads of the Department of Corrections of the fifty states and the District of Columbia. The instrument was designed to ascertain the use of ex-offenders in corrections particularly as parole and probation officers or aides. In addition, data were gathered from states employing ex-offender programs on their date of inception, the number of ex-offenders authorized and actually employed, the source and amount of funding, as well as the desirability of employing ex-offenders as parole or probation officer aides and the major advantages and disadvantages of such programs. (A copy of the questionnaire is in the appendix.) Results of this survey will be discussed in more detail later in Chapter 6.

Summary

In order to evaluate the effectiveness of ex-offenders employed as parole officer aides, the following approaches were utilized:

1. Administration of a questionnaire to parole officer aides and parole officers to measure attitudes and orientations associated with effective social service personnel;
2. In-depth interviews with parole officer aides;
3. Field observation of parole officer aides and parole officers;
4. Evaluations of parole officer aides and parole officers by unit supervisors;
5. Administration of a questionnaire to inmates in prerelease programs concerning the appropriateness of the Parole Officer Aide Program;
6. Questionnaire survey of parolees assigned to both parole officer aides and parole officers concerning the amount and quality of the supervision received.

In addition in 1974, data were collected on similar programs in the fifty states and the District of Columbia.

The questionnaire administered to parole officer aides and parole officers to measure attitudes and orientations elicited information concerning social biographical characteristics, achievement motivation, self-esteem, focal concerns, anomia, powerlessness, conservatism, dogmatism, empathy, and orientations toward corrections and causes of crime.

An on-the-job, in-depth interview was conducted by a professional interviewer with each of the parole officer aides during the first evaluation year. The focus of these interviews was to ascertain how well the parole aide was functioning, and whether or not he had been fully assimilated into the program.

Field observations conducted both years by trained university students were necessary to evaluate the activities and how time was allotted for the various activities. At this point a control group of parole officers—one officer with the least amount of work experience in the department from each unit where a parole officer aide had been placed—was selected to be used for comparative purposes. The students were assigned to work an entire day with either a parole officer aide or a parole officer from the control group.

Interviews with unit supervisors were conducted both evaluation years. The supervisors were asked specific questions concerning both the parole officer aide and parole officer in the control group working in his unit, in an effort to evaluate each one's effectiveness.

Inmates participating in a prerelease program at Ohio's adult penal institutions were administered questionnaires both years concerning the appropriateness of the Parole Officer Aide Program.

A sample of parolees under the supervision of the parole officer aides and parole officers in the control group was surveyed both years concerning their attitudes and evaluations of the services rendered. Again, this was an effort to evaluate the effectiveness of the parole officer aides in comparison to the control group.

Finally, during the second year a national survey of State Directors of Correction was conducted to determine the prevalence and desirability of ex-offender programs in corrections.

4

Attitudes and Orientations of Parole Officers in Comparison to Aides, Aides' Evaluation of Their Own Work, and Work Patterns of Officers and Aides

This chapter selectively discusses the first three approaches utilized in evaluating the Parole Officer Aide Program as outlined in Chapter 3, namely: the attitudinal questionnaire, the in-depth interviews with aides, and the data gathered from working with the officers and aides.

The Attitudinal Questionnaire

The attitudinal questionnaire measured various attitudinal and personality components often associated with more successful social workers or caseworkers (i.e., people in the helping professions). The primary focus of the evaluation was to determine how parole officer aides compare to parole officers in potential effectiveness as measured by these various scales. Table 4-1 presents the average score for aides and parole officers on each of the scales.

Motivation Scale

The first scale in Table 4-1, achievement motivation, purports to measure an individual's "desire or tendency to do things as rapidly and/or as well as possible."[1] The higher the score the more highly motivated a person is supposed to be. The average parole officer aide's score on the achievement motivation scale was only slightly higher each year than the average parole officer's score. Perhaps the justification for aides having higher motivation scores may be simply a function of the newness or novelty of a new job. Some research in the past has indicated that an employee's motivation is inversely related to the length of time on the same job.[2]

In order to determine if a parole officer's motivation was a function of the length of time employed by the Adult Parole Authority, parole officers were divided into three groups, according to the length of their service. Group 1 was composed of officers with less than one year's service, Group 2 consisted of officers employed at least one year but less than three, and Group 3 included officers employed for three or more years. Table 4-2 presents the average score for each of these groups on achievement motivation and subsequent scales to be discussed.

Comparing officers with two years' experience or less to parole officer aides

Table 4-1

Average Score for Parole Officer Aides and Parole Officers on Nine Separate Scales

Scales	1973 Respondents		1974 Respondents	
	Parole Officer Aides	Parole Officers	Parole Officer Aides	Parole Officers
	$\bar{X}$	$\bar{X}$	$\bar{X}$	$\bar{X}$
Achievement motivation scale	39.7	38.0	38.3	38.0
Self-esteem scale	44.2	43.6	44.3	44.2
Focal concerns scale	33.2	32.1	35.8	33.9
Parole aide scale	135.9	116.1	139.3	124.9
Anomia scale	2.3	2.5	1.8	3.2
Powerlessness scale	1.5	2.9	2.3	2.5
Conservatism scale	6.8	5.9	5.7	7.0
Dogmatism scale (Schulze)	27.2	26.9	26.5	29.6
Dogmatism scale (Troldahl and Powell)	44.2	41.4	41.8	46.3

indicates very little difference between the two groups with respect to motivation. Parole officers with two years' experience or less have higher motivation scores on the average than other parole officers, and only slightly lower scores than aides.

Self-Esteem Scale

The second scale in Table 4-1, self-esteem, is designed to measure how positively one thinks about himself. This scale has been correlated with an individual's self-concept, happiness, and self-confidence.[3] The assumption is that individuals who are happy, self-confident, and in possession of a positive self-concept will be more effective in working with parolees or other clients.

The data in Table 4-1 indicate that aides have slightly higher average scores both years than parole officers on self-esteem. This slight difference does not appear to be a function of length of time working for the Adult Parole Authority, inasmuch as those parole officers working two years or less have slightly lower scores on self-esteem than do other parole officers (Table 4-2).

Focal Concerns

The focal concerns scale is intended to reflect the degree of articulated commitment to norms of middle-class propriety, as opposed to lower-class

Table 4-2
Average Scores of Parole Officers on Nine Scales by Length of Service in the Adult Parole Authority

Scales	1 Year or Less		1-2 Years		3 or More Years	
	Average Score	Number of Responses	Average Score	Number of Responses	Average Score	Number of Responses
Achievement motivation scale	37.9	26	38.3	36	38.0	44
Self-esteem scale	43.8	26	44.7	35	44.3	43
Focal concern scale	33.7	26	33.5	36	34.2	44
Parole aide scale	130.4	26	124.5	36	122.2	43
Anomia scale	2.1	26	2.0	35	1.8	44
Powerlessness scale	2.2	26	2.4	36	2.7	44
Conservatism scale	7.2	25	6.5	34	7.2	43
Dogmatism scale (Schulze)	26.9	26	27.8	37	32.1	43
Dogmatism scale (Troldahl and Powell)	42.3	26	45.1	35	49.5	41

norms of "toughness," "trouble," "excitement," and reliance on "fate."[4] Contrasted with these concerns of the lower class are others that are considered more indigenous to middle-class America. That is, middle-class focal concerns are purported to deal more with cultivation of manners than with "trouble," more with control of physical aggression than with "toughness." Further, the middle class, it is argued, is more concerned with the postponement of gratification than with machinations of fate. The importance of such "concerns," if underscored by Miller's contention that the acting out of lower-class focal concerns almost inevitably runs the individual afoul of the law, is obvious. The assumption is that the higher an individual's score on the focal concerns scale, the more likely he is to subscribe to middle-class norms and the less likely he is to run afoul of the law.

Aides' and parole officers' average scores on focal concerns are reported in Table 4-1. The aides' average score on focal concerns indicates that they subscribe more to middle-class values, and are therefore less likely to have legal confrontations than are parole officers. (This is somewhat similar to Catholics subscribing more to the Protestant ethic than Protestants.) The scores on the focal concerns scale certainly indicate that the aides are middle-class goal oriented regardless of their socio-economic class as measured by income, education, parents' occupation or residence. If the focal concerns scale is valid, as Miller contends, the likelihood of aides running afoul of the law does not appear to be any greater than is the likelihood for parole officers.

Parole Aide Scale

The fourth scale in Table 4-1, the parole aide scale, is designed to measure an individual's attitude toward the value of using ex-offenders as employees of the Adult Parole Authority. A high score indicates that the respondent feels that the use of parole officer aides is a good idea, and that aides will have something unique to contribute to corrections.

As might be expected, the aides' average score is considerably higher on the parole aide scale than is the parole officers' (135.9 compared to 116.1 in 1973, and 139.3 compared to 124.9 in 1974). Parole officers' opinion of the ex-offender program has, however, improved considerably. This appears to indicate more acceptance on their part of the usefulness of ex-offenders working in the area of parole. The parole officers' favorable attitude toward using ex-offenders in parole work decreases with the officers' length of service (see Table 4-2), as does the parole officer aides'. This indicates that parole officer aides apparently have much more confidence in themselves and what they have to offer parolees when they begin than after they have had a year's experience. Also, the younger parole officers (as indicated by length of employment with the Adult Parole Authority) have more confidence and commitment to the

Parole Officer Aide Program than do parole officers who have been working in the system longer.

Anomia Scale

Srole's anomia scale is to identify the degree to which individuals have been "estranged from, or made unfriendly toward, society and the culture it carries."[5] A high score on anomia is indicative of an alienated and estranged individual. The research on anomia indicates that those individuals estranged or made unfriendly toward society have a more difficult time relating to people,[6] and therefore, one may assume, would be less successful working in a social service type career.

Table 4-1 indicates that parole officer aides scored somewhat lower both years than parole officers on anomia (2.3 compared to 2.5 in 1973, and 1.8 compared to 1.9 in 1973). This suggests that aides are somewhat more integrated into and accepting of society and its culture than are parole officers. This finding is the exact opposite of what we assumed for aides who had been incarcerated for several years of their lives (4.6 years on the average for the ten aides in 1973, and 4.3 years for the twenty-three aides employed in 1974).

Powerlessness Scale

An individual's score on powerlessness is related to his perception of internal-external control.

Internal control refers to the perception of positive and/or negative events as being a consequence of one's own actions and thereby under personal control. Whereas external control refers to the perception of positive and/or negative events as being unrelated to one's own behavior in certain situations and therefore beyond control.[7]

Powerlessness, of course, would be directly related to the perception of internal control. Those scoring high on the powerlessness scale would be somewhat more alienated from society,[8] and more likely to blame their problems on forces beyond their control, than those scoring low on the powerlessness scale.

Parole officer aides had considerably lower scores on powerlessness than did parole officers the first year (1.5 compared with 2.9), and somewhat lower in 1974 as well (2.3 compared to 2.5). Parole officers with one year's service or less in parole work had scores similar to aides' (2.3 and 2.2). The longer a parole officer had served with the Adult Parole Authority, the higher his score on powerlessness. This indicates, perhaps, that when employees begin with the Adult Parole Authority, they have more confidence in their own ability to affect the outcome of various events. Conversely, the longer employees work in social service, the more deterministic they become, attributing the outcome of events to factors beyond their own control. Again, we had assumed aides would be high on powerlessness, attributing their prior legal problems with society to forces beyond their own control. However, when length of service is taken into account, there appears to be little difference between aides and parole officers on their perception of powerlessness as a dimension of alienation.

Conservatism Scale

A conservatism scale was incorporated into the questionnaire in order to compare aides and parole officers on political conservatism. Parole officer aides were somewhat more conservative (6.8 compared to 5.9) the first year, but considerably less conservative the second year (5.7 compared to 7.0). When length of parole service is taken into consideration, aides are still considerably less conservative than parole officers.

Dogmatism Scale

The dogmatism scale, as conceived by Rokeach,[9] measures individual differences in openness or closedness of belief systems. The term "dogmatism" is used to signify the extent to which an individual has an "authoritarian outlook on life, an intolerance toward those with opposing beliefs, and a sufferance of those with similar beliefs."[10] The dogmatism scale has often been used as an indicator of one's ability to empathize or tolerate differing views and attitudes.[11] The assumption is that the lower one's score on dogmatism, the greater one's ability to empathize.[12]

Parole officers' average score was somewhat lower than aides' average score on both dogmatism scales the first year (27.2 compared to 26.9; 44.2 compared to 41.4). This indicates that parole officers were somewhat more tolerant and open-minded than the first year's parole officer aides. The second year's evaluation provided exactly the opposite conclusions, with the aides having lower scores on both dogmatism scales than the parole officers (26.5 compared to 29.6; and 41.8 compared to 46.3). When length of parole service is taken into account, however, aides are somewhat more open-minded and less dogmatic. Table 4-2 indicates a direct relationship between dogmatism and length of parole service—the longer a parole officer's service, the higher his dogmatism score. Apparently, parole officers become less tolerant and empathize less as their time in parole service increases.

On the five scales specifically designed to measure traits associated with successful social service workers (i.e., achievement motivation, self-esteem, anomia, powerlessness, and dogmatism), aides' scores are in an unfavorable direction on only one scale (dogmatism) in comparison to parole officers during the first year's evaluation. Comparing aides' and parole officers' scores on these same scales the second year, aides' scores are in a more favorable direction on every scale. When the length of service is taken into consideration, aides score higher in the direction predicting success on three of the five scales the first year (achievement motivation, self-esteem, and dogmatism) and the same on the other two scales (anomia and powerlessness) as parole officers.

Certainly only a select few of the many possible scales predicting successful social service have been employed in this analysis. Had others been utilized, different conclusions might have been reached. Nevertheless, from these findings, it appears that aides as a group possess those attitudes and orientations related to successful social service work. This may be due to the careful selection procedures followed the first year in particular in recruiting ex-offenders as parole officer aides. It does, however, indicate that the feasibility exists of finding and hiring ex-offenders with attitudes and dispositions associated with successful careers in social service work.

The final portion of our attitudinal questionnaire focused on possible differences between parole officers' and parole officer aides' attitudes toward crime and punishment. It was felt that these attitudes might affect an aide's or officer's approach in dealing with parolees.

The tabulated responses of officers' and aides' attitudes concerning crime and punishment are presented in Table 4-3, for 1974 only. Some differences are readily apparent. Parole officers perceive people in Ohio as being somewhat more punitively oriented than do aides in their approach to how adult felons should be dealt with. Parole officer aides also perceive more inmates as being mentally ill, and therefore not personally responsible for their criminal behavior than do parole officers. As to the purpose of corrections, aides see reformation as a much more important goal than do parole officers (90 percent compared to 75 percent), while aides rate general deterrence as a somewhat more important factor than do parole officers (50 percent compared to 42 percent). It is somewhat surprising that ex-offenders would rate the imposing of a penalty sufficiently severe to deter others from committing crime as a valid goal for corrections today. One of the most revealing things from Table 4-3, however, is the similarity between aides' and officers' attitudes about crime and corrections.

In-depth Interviews with Parole Officer Aides

The in-depth interviews with parole officer aides were conducted primarily to ascertain any major problems aides might be having as employees of the Adult Parole Authority. One of the major focuses of the interview was therefore upon

Table 4-3

Responses to Questions Dealing with Crime and Punishment by Parole Aides and Parole Officers

	1974 Respondents			
	Parole Aides		Parole Officers	
	Number	Percentage	Number	Percentage
People in Ohio are in favor of a more lenient approach in handling convicted adult felon offenders.				
Agree	8	40.0	24	22.4
Disagree	12	60.0	83	77.6
What proportion of offenders sent to prison do you believe to be mentally ill, although not necessarily legally insane?				
Most offenders	2	10.0	9	8.5
A significant minority	13	65.0	64	60.4
None or very few	2	10.0	20	18.9
Don't know	3	15.0	13	12.3
How important is reformation in corrections today?				
Very important	13	65.0	42	39.6
Quite important	5	25.0	38	35.8
Some importance	2	10.0	19	17.9
Little importance	–	–	6	5.7
No importance	–	–	1	.9
How important should general deterrence as the purpose of corrections be?				
Very important	–	–	12	11.2
Quite important	10	50.0	33	30.8
Some importance	6	30.0	33	30.8
Little importance	4	20.0	26	24.3
No importance	–	–	3	2.8
How important should individual deterrence be?				
Very important	2	10.0	17	15.9
Quite important	8	40.0	27	25.2
Some importance	7	35.0	40	37.4
Little importance	3	15.0	20	18.7
No importance	–	–	3	2.8

Table 4-3 (cont.)

	1974 Respondents			
	Parole Aides		Parole Officers	
	Number	Percentage	Number	Percentage
How important should punishment be?				
Very important	3	15.0	11	10.5
Quite important	5	25.0	13	12.4
Some importance	7	35.0	48	45.7
Little importance	3	15.0	23	21.9
No importance	2	10.0	10	9.5
How important should incapacitation be?				
Very important	3	15.0	16	15.0
Quite important	6	30.0	21	19.6
Some importance	9	45.0	50	46.7
Little importance	2	10.0	17	15.9
No importance	–	–	3	2.8
What conclusions have you reached concerning the causes of crime from your observations of offenders?				
Situational factors society, kicks, excitement	4	23.5	28	28.3
Biological factors heredity, minority groups, mental deficiency	3	17.6	7	7.1
Lower-class, poor, poorly educated, irresponsible parents, bad marriage	8	47.1	59	59.6
Chemical substances drugs, alcohol	2	11.8	5	5.1

job satisfaction. As can be seen from Table 4-4, the majority of aides were very satisfied with their work. All but one of the aides felt that their duties and responsibilities were clearly defined. The proportion of an aide's work that was closely supervised varied substantially, with some receiving very little supervision (3, or 30 percent) and others (4, or 40 percent) having almost all of their work supervised.

The aides' responses to questions concerning their work satisfaction are presented in Table 4-5. Again, most aides were very satisfied with their fellow workers (8, or 80 percent), and only one was very dissatisfied with his colleagues. Most of the men were also very satisfied with their supervisors (8, or 80 percent) and nine of the ten aides indicated that their colleagues had

Table 4-4

Responses to Questions Dealing with Parole Officer Aides' Attitudes Toward Their Occupation

	Number	Percentage
For what proportion of your work are you directly accountable to someone else?		
No supervision	0	0.0
Very little	3	30.0
One-fourth	1	10.0
Half	0	0.0
Three-fourths	2	20.0
Almost all	4	40.0
How clearly defined are your duties and responsibilities?		
As clearly as they should be	9	90.0
Almost as clearly as they should be	1	10.0
Should be defined somewhat more clearly	0	0.0
Should be defined much more clearly	0	0.0
How satisfied are you with your present job?		
Very dissatisfied	1	10.0
Slightly dissatisfied	0	0.0
Neutral	0	0.0
Moderately satisfied	2	20.0
Very satisfied	7	70.0

welcomed them and made them feel like important employees of the Adult Parole Authority. We were somewhat surprised at the aides' work satisfaction and apparent acceptance by other employees of the Parole Department, given the personal doubts these employees had concerning the aide program, as was indicated by our attitudinal survey reported above (see Tables 4-1 and 4-2, the parole aide scale). Nevertheless, the aides seemed to feel accepted and are extremely pleased with their work, with the exception of one. The one indicator used in the 1974 evaluation of job satisfaction is a question that asked aides and officers: "Do you plan to make a career of correctional work?" All of the aides responded "yes," in comparison to 78 percent of the parole officers. The aides, we assume, must therefore still be finding job satisfaction and be committed to their work.

Several open-ended questions attempted to ascertain what aides felt should be done to better the parole aide program. Seven of the ten aides felt they would be more efficient if given more authority. The main justification was to expedite

Table 4-5

Responses to Questions Dealing with Parole Officer Aides' Satisfaction with Their Work Situation

	Number	Percentage
How satisfied are you with your fellow workers?		
Very dissatisfied	1	10.0
Slightly dissatisfied	0	0.0
Neutral	0	0.0
Moderately satisfied	0	0.0
Very satisfied	8	80.0
Don't know, not applicable	1	10.0
How satisfied are you with your present supervisor?		
Very dissatisfied	1	10.0
Slightly dissatisfied	0	0.0
Neutral	0	0.0
Moderately satisfied	1	10.0
Very satisfied	8	80.0
Don't know, not applicable	0	0.0
How satisfied are you with the amount of freedom you have in your job?		
Very dissatisfied	1	10.0
Slightly dissatisfied	1	10.0
Neutral	1	10.0
Moderately satisfied	3	30.0
Very satisfied	4	40.0
Don't know, not applicable	0	0.0
To what extent do the people in your office make you feel like an important member of the "parole team"?		
Not at all	0	0.0
To a small extent	0	0.0
To a fair extent	0	0.0
To a great extent	9	90.0
Don't know, not applicable	1	10.0

matters such as "holds" or "parole revocations," although some aides indicated that more authority would simply be an indication on the part of the Adult Parole Authority (APA) that they trusted aides as much as they do parole officers.

In response to the question, "Why do you continue to work for the APA?" almost all aides responded very positively. Typical answers were: "I love the work," "I like meeting and helping people," "It makes me feel good." The only recurring complaint aides had about their job was the low pay they received. Nevertheless, the majority did not feel that they should be making as much as parole officers, because of the officers' more extensive training.

Every aide seemed to feel that he was really helping parolees. Nevertheless, only five aides indicated that they were more effective than parole officers, while four felt that aides were equally as effective. Although the aides had considerable confidence in their ability to help parolees, only four felt being an ex-offender was more important than being a community resident in working with parolees. The apparent reason is that aides saw their main job as that of helping parolees find jobs. Aides indicated that being an ex-offender does not hinder one in helping parolees find jobs, but not being from the community limits one's job resources. Next to assisting parolees in finding employment, aides felt that their main task was acting as "go-between" or mediator between parolees and parole officers.

All of the aides felt that the initial training seminars were not only very helpful but essential. The topics covered in the seminar that the aides found to be most helpful were those concerning counseling techniques and report writing. The one major problem several aides mentioned dealt with report writing. They felt that this area should be stressed at subsequent training seminars.

Parole aides' responses to several questions dealing with parolees and parole procedures are tabulated in Table 4-6. All aides indicated that it would be beneficial if parole officers had smaller caseloads, so that the average offender released from prison would have more help succeeding on parole. The majority (7, or 70 percent) of the aides also favored the use of volunteers to assist parole officers with their parolees.

Parole aides' responses to questions dealing with crime and the law are tabulated in Table 4-7. The majority of aides who responded felt that the Ohio laws are too restrictive and punitive. Nevertheless, aides were almost evenly divided over the proper use of the death penalty; four felt it should be used more often, while five felt it should be abolished. Eight of the ten aides rated crime as Ohio's most serious problem.

Parole aides' responses to the adequacy of state correctional personnel is recorded in Table 4-8. These responses are interesting in that only two (20 percent) of the aides rated state juvenile correctional workers as doing a reasonably good job or better, while at the same time eight (80 percent) of the aides rate state adult correctional workers as performing reasonably well or better. Perhaps these responses more than anything else indicate how well most aides are integrated into the Adult Parole Authority and how they have adopted the Adult Parole Authority's point of view.

Table 4-6

Responses to Questions Dealing with Parolees and Parole Procedures by Parole Officer Aides

	Number	Percentage
The average prisoner released from prison should make it on his own without subsequent help		
Agree	1	10.0
Disagree	9	90.0
The average prisoner released from prison on parole needs some help to succeed on parole		
Agree	10	100.0
Disagree	0	0.0
A parolee should work things out alone and not be "bugged" by a parole officer		
Agree	2	20.0
Disagree	6	60.0
Not sure	1	10.0
Don't know, not applicable	1	10.0
It would be beneficial if the average parole officer had a smaller caseload		
Agree	10	100.0
Disagree	0	0.0
It would be beneficial if Ohio utilized volunteers to assist parole officers with their parolees		
Agree	7	70.0
Disagree	3	30.0

Work Patterns of Parole Officers and Parole Aides

Information gathered by the undergraduate students during the day they spent with parole officers and parole officer aides can best be analyzed by separating it into three separate categories: a description of the number and type of contacts with parolees, an estimate of time spent engaged in various activities, frequency distributions of the quality of relationships parole officers and aides had with both parolees and fellow workers. The observations made during 1973 and 1974 will be combined in the tables and text for better conceptualization and clarity.

Table 4-7

Responses to Questions Dealing with Crime and Criminal Law in Ohio by Parole Officer Aides

	Number	Percentage
Do you feel laws dealing with criminal offenses in Ohio are too lenient, too severe, or about right?		
Too lenient	1	10.0
About right	0	0.0
Too severe	4	40.0
Don't know, no opinion	0	0.0
Not applicable	5	50.0
Should the death penalty be used more often than it is now, less often than now, or be abolished?		
More often	4	40.0
As often as now	0	0.0
Less often	0	0.0
Abolished	5	50.0
Don't know, no opinion	1	10.0
How serious do you feel the crime problem in Ohio is?		
Not very serious	0	0.0
Quite serious	1	10.0
Most serious problem in Ohio	8	80.0
Don't know, not applicable	1	10.0

Of the twenty original students assigned to spend one day in the field with the aides and officers the first year, nineteen completed their assignment; one student moved immediately, and his report was not received. Also, some student observers failed to record all the information desired; thus, the N (or number of respondents) may vary from table to table.

Numbers and Types of Contacts

According to Figure 4-1, the number of contacts both officers and aides had with parolees during the one work day varied from a minimum of one contact to a maximum of thirteen. The average number of parolees seen during a day is somewhat higher for parole officers than aides. This may be expected, inasmuch as parole officers' average caseload is over twice the size of the aides'. In

Table 4-8
**Responses to Questions Dealing with State Correctional Personnel by Parole
Officer Aides**

	Number	Percentage
How well are state juvenile correctional workers doing their job?		
Very well	1	10.0
Reasonably well	1	10.0
Somewhat poorly	2	20.0
Very poorly	2	20.0
Don't know, not applicable	4	40.0
How well are state adult correctional workers doing their job?		
Very well	4	40.0
Reasonably well	4	40.0
Somewhat poorly	0	0.0
Very poorly	1	10.0
Don't know, not applicable	1	10.0

addition, several aides spent only 50 percent of the day in the field, due to such
factors as attending college classes in the morning and coordinating job-place-
ment programs. In addition one aide had been seriously ill, and consequently
had only five parolees to supervise. When these factors are taken into account,
there seems to be little difference in the frequency of visits. Interestingly, parole
officers' and aides' average number of visits increased in 1974 when compared to
the initial evaluation in 1973. The first year, the parole officers on the average
saw 4.1 parolees during the students' visit, in comparison to 2.9 for the aides.
During the 1974 visits, parole officers saw an average of 5.5 parolees, compared
to 5.3 for the aides. The number of contacts calculated by the students is also
not necessarily indicative of the number of contacts made by an aide or officer
on a typical day. However, the figures were often verified as typical by
comments from the aides and officers to the students.

Time Spent in Various Activities

Table 4-9 shows the percentage range of time spent engaged in various activities
for the group of parole officers and group of parole aides. Mean scores for the
two groups indicate that both spend about the same percentage of time with
parolees. There was a considerable difference in the average amount of time
aides and officers spent writing reports or recording data during the first year's

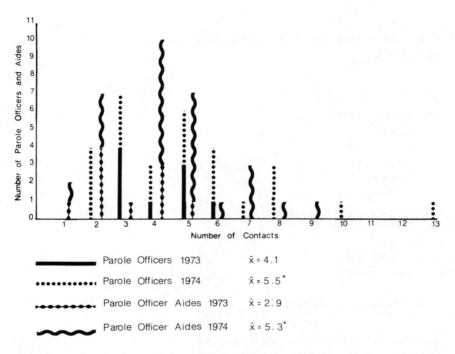

*The means for 1974 are based on work days in the field. Five of the 23 aides had other responsibilities the entire morning (e.g. job placement program, release time for school, etc.) while only 1 of the 21 parole officers had such other responsibilities for one-half day. The averages are therefore based on 20.5 work days for both the parole officers and the parole officer aides.

Figure 4-1. Number of Parolees Seen in Working Day as Reported by Student Field Workers

evaluation (17 percent versus 5 percent), but presently these differences seem to be minimal. Aides apparently had considerable problems in writing satisfactory reports the first year, but the additional training in dictating and report writing received the second year may be responsible for the equal time students found aides and parole officers working on reports the following year.

The category "other" shows a wide range of time spent in activities other than those specified. Some of these activities included visiting halfway houses, job training programs, meeting with prospective employers or relatives of parolees, placing phone calls and delivering mail (a specific job given to aides in some offices). One parole aide spent a half day lecturing to a group of high school students; one parole officer spent a half day target practicing; and some of the total time for each officer or aide was spent in educating the visiting student on various parole matters.

Table 4-9

Percentage of Time Allotted for Various Activities During Day as Reported by Student Field Workers (1973 and 1974 Responses Combined)

	Range		Mean	
	Parole Officer Aide	Parole Officer	Parole Officer Aide	Parole Officer
With parolees	15-75%	7-70%	36%	35%
Traveling	10-50%	12-60%	28%	32%
Writing reports or recording data	0-30%	0-24%	11%	11%
Meetings	0-55%[a]	0-20%	15%[a]	8%
Other	0-50%	0-60%	10%	14%

[a]Only one student mentioned his parole officer spending one-half day in a meeting; the 15 percent average is perhaps inflated.

Quality of Relationships with
Parolees and Fellow Workers

Figure 4-2 shows the frequency distribution of students' views on the quality of the relationship observed between the parole officer or aide and the parolees on his caseload. Parole officer aides were evaluated better in relating and working with parolees than were parole officers, although both were viewed as being very effective. Both years, students have ranked the aides as working and relating better with their parolees. The 1974 student evaluation gave eighteen aides excellent ratings in evaluating their work with parolees, while nine of the parole officers received this highest ranking.

The frequency distribution for the quality of relationship parole officers and aides had with fellow staff members is shown in Figure 4-3. There is no difference in the students' overall evaluation of aides' and officers' relationship with fellow workers. Sixteen officers were rated as having "excellent" relations with fellow workers, as were sixteen aides. This does indicate that ex-offenders apparently can work in parole agencies and be accepted by fellow workers. Many have voiced concern about possible resistance to the paraprofessional by professional officers. The evaluation of the ex-offender Parole Officer Aide Program in Ohio does not reflect evidence to justify this concern.

The student workers in 1974 were also asked to evaluate the parole officer or aide they worked with on the three criteria mentioned repeatedly by parole officials as necessary for being successful in working with parolees: (1) ability to motivate, (2) ability to relate, and (3) willingness to put oneself out in helping parolees. Table 4-10 reports the students' ranking of aides and officers on these three criteria. Aides and officers were ranked approximately the same with

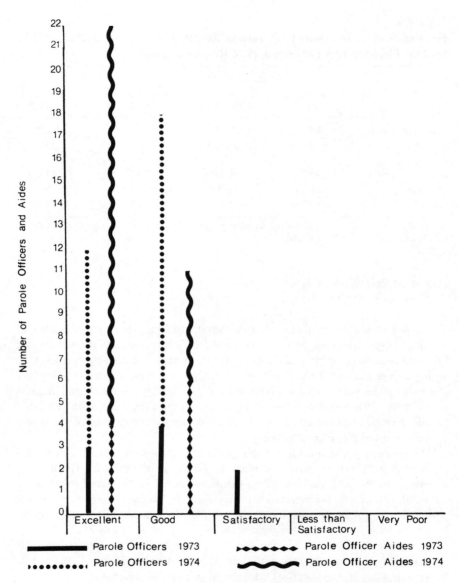

Figure 4-2. Quality of Relationships with Parolees of Parole Officers and Aides as Reported by Student Field Workers

*The means for 1974 are based on work days in the field. Five of the 23 aides had other responsibilities the entire morning (e.g. job placement program, release time for school, etc.) while only 1 of the 21 parole officers had such other responsibilities for one-half day. The averages are therefore based on 20.5 work days for both the parole officers and the parole officer aides.

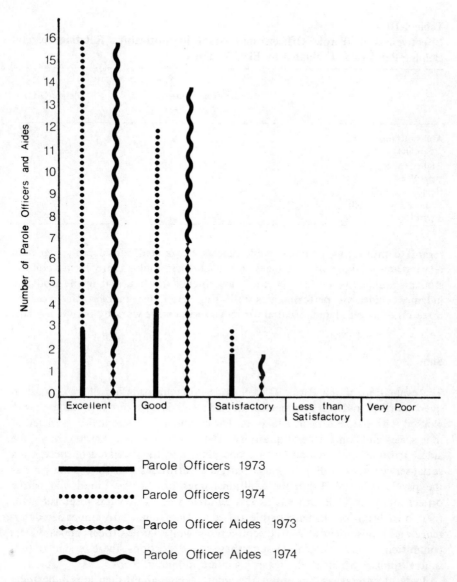

*The means for 1974 are based on work days in the field. Five of the 23 aides had other responsibilities the entire morning (e.g. job placement program, release time for school, etc.) while only 1 of the 21 parole officers had such other responsibilities for one-half day. The averages are therefore based on 20.5 work days for both the parole officers and the parole officer aides.

Figure 4-3. Quality of Relationships with Fellow Workers as Evaluated by Student Field Workers

Table 4-10

Effectiveness of Parole Officers and Aides in Motivating, Relating to, and Helping Parolees as Evaluated by Field Workers

| | 1974 Respondents | |
| | Parole Officer Aides | Parole Officers |
	$\bar{X}$	$\bar{X}$
Ability to motivate parolees	75.7	77.3
Ability to relate to parolees	90.7	85.6
Willingness to put himself out or help parolees	89.1	83.9

regard to motivating parolees, while aides were ranked considerably higher in relating and working with parolees. Although these rankings are based upon the students' subjective evaluation, they nevertheless indicate that in the students' judgment, aides are performing as well as or better than parole officers on the three criteria considered essential for social service type work by parole officials.

Summary

The evaluation of the Parole Officer Aide Program made use of an attitudinal questionnaire, in-depth interviews with aides, and data gathered by students who worked with parole officers and aides. The attitudinal questionnaire consisted of nine scales and some general questions. The scales indicated that in general, the aides' attitudes and orientations are very similar to those related to success as a social-service worker. For the most part, their attitudes were nearly the same as the parole officers'. From the additional questions, it was found that parole officer aides see Ohio citizens as less punitive and inmates less responsible for their own behavior than do parole officers. Aides tended to emphasize deterrence and punishment as goals of corrections, while parole officers appeared less committed to any one goal. Despite these few exceptions, there tended to be a general similarity in attitudes regarding crime and punishment.

In-depth interviews concerning the aides' feelings about their jobs indicated a general satisfaction with their work and a feeling that they were accepted by other employees. A recurring complaint from the aides, however, was the low pay that they received. All of the aides also suggested that more authority be given them in their work. They felt, however, that adult correctional workers were doing a good job. Concerning parole procedures, aides suggested that parole officers should have smaller caseloads, and that more volunteers should be used to assist them. It was found that the parole officers' and aides' average number of visits increased in 1974 when compared to the initial evaluation of 1973. While the officers' $\overline{X}$ was substantially higher than the aides' $\overline{X}$ in 1973, there was only a slight difference in 1974.

Aides and officers spent their time in reasonably similar ways, with the one exception that aides spent significantly more time on report writing during the first year's evaluation and in meetings the second year. Parole officer aides were ranked slightly higher than parole officers on the quality of relationships with parolees and on the ability to relate to and work with parolees. There was no difference in the students' overall evaluation of aides' and officers' relationships with fellow workers.

5

The Findings: Data on Supervisors', Inmates', and Parolees' Attitudes Concerning Parole Officer Aides

In this chapter, three additional approaches utilized in evaluating the Parole Officer Aide Program are described. First, the information obtained from interviewing each parole supervisor who had an aide working in his unit will be discussed. Second, data about the program obtained from questionnaires administered to inmates participating in a prerelease program will be presented. Finally, data obtained from a survey of parolees under the supervision of aides and officers will be examined.

Unit Supervisors' Evaluations

Each unit supervisor was individually interviewed by a member of the research program and asked to rank first the parole officer aide (POA) or the "control" parole officer (PO) on several characteristics. After the supervisor had ranked either the parole officer or the aide, he was then asked to rank the other on the same characteristics.

The average score for parole officers and parole officer aides as ranked by unit supervisors is given in Table 5-1. Supervisors rated parole officers higher on their ability both to motivate and relate to parolees in 1973, while aides were ranked higher in 1973 on their willingness to "go the extra mile" or put themselves out in working with parolees. These first three characteristics were most often mentioned as necessary for a parole officer to perform well on his job. If the three scales are treated as separate indicators of an underlying dimension and the assumption is made that they are additive, parole officers would be ranked overall somewhat higher in 1973 as good social service workers (223 as compared to 219). However, supervisors in 1974 rated parole officers higher on all three of these indicators, as well as the other five criteria reported in Table 5-1. In fact, aides' ratings in 1974 are not only lower than parole officers' on every indicator as rated by supervisors, but are lower as well on every indicator than the 1973 aides'. This led the researchers to compare first and second year aides' scores on each indicator (see Table 5-2). The aides hired in 1972-73 had higher scores on every indicator than the aides hired in 1973-74. The scores of the first group of aides were very comparable to the average parole officer's score. In fact, aides hired in 1972 received higher scores on three of the first four indicators than did the parole officers. They were overall very comparable to parole officers, with one exception, report writing, in which officers still excelled.

59

Table 5-1
Unit Supervisors' Ranking of Parole Officers and Parole Officer Aides on Several Indicators

	1973 Respondents		1974 Respondents	
	Parole Officer Aides $\bar{X}$ Score	Parole Officers $\bar{X}$ Score	Parole Officer Aides $\bar{X}$ Score	Parole Officers $\bar{X}$ Score
Ability to motivate parolees	63.0	69.0	61.0	66.5
Ability to relate to parolees	71.0	73.0	65.2	70.0
Willingness to put himself out	85.0	81.0	72.4	76.5
Getting jobs or job training for parolees	73.0	69.0	66.2	68.7
Relating and getting along with fellow workers	86.0	86.0	73.3	79.6
Relating and getting along with representatives of other programs and agencies in the community	77.0	80.0	72.4	78.3
Report writing	53.0	75.0	52.4	73.9
Overall as an employee of the Adult Parole Authority	65.0	78.0	62.9	75.5

The only other characteristic in 1973 on which supervisors rated aides better than parole officers was in getting jobs or job training for parolees ($\overline{X}$ of 73 compared to a $\overline{X}$ of 69). Somewhat surprising to the evaluation staff was the fact that the aides hired during the first year of the program were rated on an equal level with parole officers in their ability to relate and get along with fellow workers during both evaluation periods. Although this is consistent with the aides' own evaluation of their being accepted and made to feel an important part of the parole team (as reported in the section on in-depth interviews with parole aides), the evaluators felt that there might be considerable resistance on the part of the parole officer to accepting ex-offenders as colleagues.

Supervisors rated aides somewhat lower than parole officers in getting along with representatives of other programs and agencies in the community ($\overline{X}$ of 77 compared to a $\overline{X}$ of 80 in 1973 and 72.4 compared to 78.3 in 1974). This difference appears to be a function of the problems aides have had in being accepted as bonafide employees of the Adult Parole Authority by the local police. Several supervisors indicated that the police had numerous reservations about using ex-offenders as state employees, but their resistance appeared to be diminishing. Aides also reported in our in-depth interviews that the police frequently refused to cooperate or share information with them unless a parole officer was also present.

Supervisors rated parole officers considerably higher than aides both in report-writing skills and overall as employees. However, when one compares supervisors' evaluation of aides who have worked for the APA more than a year with parole officers as overall employees, there is no difference in their ratings

Table 5-2

Unit Supervisors' Ranking of Parole Officer Aides on Several Indicators by Length of Service in the Adult Parole Authority

	1 Year or Less Average Score	1 - 2 Years Average Score
Ability to motivate parolees	57.3	63.0
Ability to relate to parolees	57.3	72.0
Willingness to put himself out	68.6	76.6
Getting jobs or job training for parolees	62.7	69.5
Relating and getting along with fellow workers	69.1	77.5
Relating and getting along with representatives of other programs and agencies in the community	66.8	77.0
Report writing	48.2	56.5
Overall as an employee of the Adult Parole Authority	58.2	67.0

(75.5 versus 75.5). In other words, aides who are now in their second year of work with the APA are rated overall as valuable as the average parole officer. The aides indicated in our 1973 interviews that one of their major problems was report writing. Supervisors are apparently aware of this deficiency, inasmuch as the greatest difference between their rating of aides and parole officers was on report writing (22 points both years). Aides now in their second year of employment with the APA appear to have reduced this deficiency somewhat, but are still ranked seventeen points lower in report-writing ability than parole officers.

A number of questions were asked each supervisor concerning his evaluation of the Parole Officer Aide Program. Tabulated responses to these questions are given in Table 5-3. Supervisors were asked how often the aide in their unit spoke at public gatherings as a representative of the Adult Parole Authority and how valuable he (the supervisor) felt this function was. The responses varied significantly. The number of public speeches made in the preceding six months ranged from 0 to 48, with the average being 9 during 1973 and 13 in 1974. Most supervisors indicated that such public speaking was a valuable function. Supervisors who rated such public speaking as valuable often added that it helped the aides acquire status and respectability. Such comments were interpreted as indicating that some supervisors, at least, may have rated public speaking for aides as a valuable function of the program more in terms of offering the aide an opportunity for personal growth and advancement than as a valuable function for the Adult Parole Authority per se. A typical supervisor's comment on aides' public speaking was: "I think it is a very valuable function to have aides represent the APA by giving talks in our schools and to public groups. It gives people in the community an idea of what we're doing and what we're trying to do." Another commented: "Having aides give talks is extremely valuable to the APA. Aides are more believable; they are also generally perceived as being more sincere—they know what it's like." At least one supervisor felt that the aides' public speaking was only an extension of Operation Prevention (a program which uses ex-inmates as public speakers in schools), and therefore nothing new or that valuable. None of the supervisors mentioned aides' public speaking as the major advantage of the Parole Aide Program.

The most commonly mentioned advantage of the Parole Officer Aide Program is the function the aides serve as a source of knowledge for other parole officers. In this respect, aides appear to understand many of the problems parolees are having and what, if anything, can be done to help them. The second most commonly mentioned advantage of the aide program according to supervisors is that aides teach the other parole officers how to relate to parolees. This was mentioned by several supervisors as an invaluable aid. Several supervisors mentioned that if the program were ever terminated, the APA should

Table 5-3
Unit Supervisors' Evaluation of the Parole Officer Aide Program

	1973 Respondents		1974 Respondents	
	Mean/ 6 Months	Range/ 6 Months	Mean/ 6 Months	Range/ 6 Months
How many times has the aide in your unit spoken as a representative of the Adult Parole Authority in the last 6 months?	9.2	1-36	13.0	0-48
	N	Percent	N	Percent
How valuable a function is having aides speak as representatives of the Adult Parole Authority?				
Very valuable	4	40%	12	60%
Valuable	3	30%	6	30%
Not that valuable	3	30%	1	5%
No answer	–	–	1	5%
The major advantage of the Parole Officer Aides Program:				
Source of information for parole officers (mediator)	5	50%[a]	5	25%
Teaches us how to relate to parolees	4	40%	9	45%
Better equipped to develop employment	2	20%	2	10%
Can relate and handle some parolees that other parole officers can't reach	2	20%	1	5%
Sets good example for parolee	–	–	2	10%
The major disadvantage of the Parole Officer Aides Program:				
Lack of cooperation police provide aides	3	30%	8	40%[a]
Aides' lack of education	3	30%	5	25%
None	2	20%	2	10%
Concern they may go bad and cast a bad reflection on the Adult Parole Authority	1	10%	1	5%
Aides' lack of authority	1	10%	5	25%

[a]These figures add to more than 100% because some supervisors gave more than one major advantage or disadvantage.

retain the aides as consultants, because of their insight and knowledge. Another supervisor remarked that "every parole office should have at lease one aide as a reference source." Other advantages of the aide program commonly mentioned by supervisors were the good example that aides set for parolees and the ability aides had in securing employment for parolees. One supervisor remarked that the aide in his unit had such a knack of securing jobs for parolees that several parole officers had him (the aide) help them get jobs for their parolees.

When questioned concerning the major disadvantages of the Parole Officer Aide Program, supervisors most frequently mentioned the policemen's lack of cooperation with aides and the aides' limited education. Other supervisors, while acknowledging the problem aides have because of their limited education, felt that their limited formal education might be an advantage in helping them to relate to most parolees. The aides' lack of authority (i.e., to arrest and violate parolees) was also mentioned as a disadvantage of the program.

Nine of the ten supervisors interviewed the first year and nineteen of the twenty interviewed the second year were very pleased with the Parole Officer Aide Program. The following are some typical responses by unit supervisors:

I wasn't for it [the program] to begin with but it has been most successful. [The aide] knows where to find the bodies and teaches us how to relate with the parolees to develop good rapport.

He [the aide] has had success with some of my failures. There should be at least one aide in every parole office in the state.

The program should be expanded, and every parole unit should have at least one aide.

He [the aide] puts in more hours than anyone in my office. He's the most willing to put himself out of any of my men. He often works even Saturdays and Sundays.

The supervisors, as a group, felt the aide program to be one of the best innovations to come from the Adult Parole Authority in some time. Almost all unit supervisors felt that the program should be expanded and enlarged. When asked what they would do differently if they were responsible for evaluating and restructuring the program, many supervisors commented on the selection process. Several supervisors felt that parole officer aides should be more carefully selected. There were no such comments from supervisors the first year, when the project coordinator selected the aides. The second year aides were selected more by regional or unit offices, and some supervisors seem quite concerned that future selections be made more carefully. This would seem justified on the basis of scores received on several indicators by aides with less than one year's experience, in comparison with the aides selected the first year.

Inmate Attitudes Toward the Parole Officer Aide Program

The prerelease inmate populations at Lebanon and Mansfield Correctional Institutions, consisting of 64 inmates, were administered a questionnaire in

1973. In 1974, the prerelease inmate populations at Lebanon, Lucasville, London, Chillicothe, and Marion Correctional institutions, as well as the reformatories at Mansfield and Marysville, were administered questionnaires. The sample population in 1974 was comprised of 180 inmates.

Somewhat surprising to the researchers was the fact that in 1974 only 44 percent of the inmates interviewed knew anything about Ohio hiring "ex-cons" to work as parole officer aides. The Parole Officer Aide Program had been in operation over a year and a half at the time the inmates were interviewed. At the same time, 94 percent of the inmates knew about Ohio's new Shock Parole Statute, which had been passed three or four months before the interviews. Nevertheless, the inmates were very optimistic and positive about the use of ex-offenders in corrections. In fact, 79 percent agreed that the use of ex-cons as parole officers would probably result in new treatment programs for helping parolees stay out of trouble, while only 9 percent of the inmates disagreed. This seems to reflect the inmates' very positive attitudes toward the program.

Table 5-4 shows six additional questions asked both inmate populations concerning attitudes toward the parole officer aide program. (Question numbers on the tables do not necessarily correspond with those found in a copy of the questionnaire in the appendix.) Responses to question number 1 indicate that 95 percent of the inmates in 1973 and 85 percent in 1974 would prefer to have a parole officer aide rather than a parole officer supervising them upon release from prison. Only 5 percent preferred a parole officer during the first year's evaluation, while 15 percent of the second-year respondents preferred a parole officer. Nine percent were undecided. In most cases, preference would of course be based on the inmate's idea of what he would prefer rather than on the inmate's actual prior experience with an aide's supervision.

When asked if a parole officer aide would be better able to help parolees avoid problems than a regular parole officer, 86 percent answered in the affirmative in 1973 and 79 percent in 1974. Only 3 percent of the inmates in 1973 compared to 11 percent in 1974 felt that parole officers would be more helpful to parolees than aides. However, a higher percentage of inmates in 1973 indicated interest in being a parole officer aide than in 1974 (69 percent compared to 56 percent).

Sixty-nine percent of the prerelease inmates agreed that most parole officers find it hard to understand parolees' problems because the officers came from a middle-class background; 16 percent disagreed with this statement in 1973 and 26 percent in 1974. The response to this question may be an indication of one of the reasons why the majority of the inmates would rather have a parole officer aide supervising them.

Question number 5 serves as a check for question number 1. Fifty-five percent of the inmates in 1973 and 61 percent in 1974 disagreed with the statement that most parolees would object to being supervised by an aide rather than an officer. Only 22 percent agreed that most parolees would rather be under a parole officer's supervision. This 22 percent differs somewhat from the approximately 10 percent who would rather have a parole officer supervising

Table 5-4

Responses to Questions Dealing with Attitudes Toward Parole and the Parole Aide Program by Inmates of Ohio Correctional Institutions

	1973 Respondents		1974 Respondents	
	Number	%	Number	%
1. If you had your choice upon release from prison, would you prefer a parole officer or a parole officer aide?				
Parole officer	3	5.2	25	14.6
Parole officer aide	55	94.8	146	85.4
2. A parole officer aide will be better able to help parolees avoid problems than can regular parole officers.				
Strongly agree	18	28.1	64	36.8
Agree	37	57.8	74	42.5
Undecided	7	10.9	17	9.8
Disagree	2	3.1	12	6.9
Strongly disagree	0	0.0	7	4.0
3. Following release from prison and completion of parole, I would like to become a parole officer aide.				
Strongly agree	12	18.8	48	27.9
Agree	32	50.0	49	28.5
Undecided	8	12.5	31	18.2
Disagree	8	12.5	30	17.4
Strongly disagree	4	6.2	14	8.1
4. Most parole officers find it hard to understand parolees' problems because the officers come from middle-class backgrounds.				
Agree	44	68.8	97	56.4
Undecided	10	15.6	31	18.2
Disagree	10	15.6	44	25.6
5. Most parolees will object to being supervised by a parole officer aide rather than by a normal parole officer.				
Strongly agree	2	3.1	10	5.7
Agree	12	18.8	30	17.1
Undecided	15	23.4	29	16.6
Disagree	27	42.2	74	42.3
Strongly disagree	8	12.5	32	18.3

Table 5-4 (cont.)

	1973 Respondents		1974 Respondents	
	Number	%	Number	%
6. Parolees who are supervised by a parole officer aide are more likely to succeed on parole than those supervised by normal parole officers.				
Strongly agree	19	29.7	42	23.7
Agree	29	45.3	75	42.4
Undecided	13	20.3	28	15.8
Disagree	3	4.7	23	13.0
Strongly disagree	0	0.0	9	5.1

them (question number 1). Although it appears that approximately 90 percent of the inmates would prefer an aide *themselves*, they feel that only approximately one-half of the parolee population think similarly.

The responses to question number 6 indicate that although only a little over half of the parolee population may prefer a parole aide according to other inmates, these same inmates feel that parolees would fare much better under an aide's supervision. Approximately 70 percent of the prerelease population felt that parolees were more likely to succeed on parole when supervised by an aide. The percentage of inmates so responding declined, however, from 1973 to 1974 (75 percent to 66 percent).

The inmates evaluated the Parole Officer Aide Program very highly. The majority indicated a preference for an aide to supervise them upon release. They felt as a group that an aide's background and experience would be beneficial in understanding, helping, and working with parolees. However, comparing 1973 and 1974 replies, one notes a more critical evaluation of the aide program by inmates during the second year. This more critical evaluation is similar to the change noted in 1973 between inmates' and parolees' attitudes toward the program. In 1973, inmates were much more optimistic about the benefits of having an ex-offender parole officer than were parolees. It may well be that as inmates and parolees become more acquainted with the parole officer aide program, they realize that the aides are employees of the Adult Parole Authority and define their work accordingly. Although aides appear to be more liberal and perhaps innovative in working with parolees, nevertheless, they also subscribe to APA standards and expectations of their work. Overall, however, reactions to the Parole Aide Program were extremely positive both years. The majority of inmates would prefer to be supervised by an aide, feel an aide is better able to understand their problems, and would enjoy the opportunity to be employed as an aide.

Survey of Parolees

The next approach utilized in evaluating the Parole Officer Aide Program was a survey of parolees being supervised by either a parole officer or an aide. The results of this evaluative approach should be as valid and meaningful as any of the other techniques utilized, or even more so. This is particularly the case inasmuch as aides and parole officers are employed to help parolees. The parolees themselves are perhaps more qualified than anyone to evaluate the quantity and quality of help they are receiving from their aides or officers. The high return rate of the questionnaires also allows one to have substantial confidence that the results obtained are fairly representative of Ohio's parolees.

The parolees' responses to questions concerning their experiences with and attitudes toward parole officers and parole officer aides is given in Table 5-5. Parolees supervised by an aide indicate that they can communicate better with him than do parolees supervised by a parole officer (94 percent compared to 80 percent in 1973 and 90 percent compared to 87 percent in 1974). Parolees working with aides also reported more frequently that they could trust them than did parolees working with officers in 1973 (83 percent compared to 77 percent), but this trend is reversed in 1974 (78 percent compared to 82 percent). A greater percentage of parolees supervised by an aide indicated that he cared more about what they said and did than did parolees supervised by a parole officer (95 percent versus 87 percent in 1973 and 94 percent versus 91 percent in 1974). The data from parolees is inconclusive as to whether aides or officers are less likely to be "conned." Parolees in the first year's evaluation reported less "conning" of their aides than those being supervised by a parole officer. The exact opposite pattern is observed from the 1974 data—unless the researchers themselves are being conned! Parolees supervised by aides responded affirmatively much more often than those supervised by officers to the statement: "Do other parolees assigned to your parole officer feel he is doing a good job?" (35 percent versus 18 percent in 1972, and 30 percent versus 23 percent in 1974).

Aides were rated as being generally more helpful, concerned, and understanding than parole officers. However, in response to the question, "Would your parole officer do more for you than is required?" parolees supervised by parole officers were more likely to respond affirmatively in 1974 (77 percent) than those supervised by aides (70 percent). This is a definite reversal from the first year of the parole officer aide program, when aides were rated considerably more helpful than parole officers. Aides were rated significantly higher than officers in terms of having connections to help parolees get jobs both years (61 percent compared with 46 percent in 1973, and 55 percent versus 43 percent in 1974). Aides were understandably rated better both years at comprehending what it is like to be on parole.

The first year parolees felt that aides were considerably easier than parole officers to find if they needed them. Certainly the ease with which parolees can

Table 5-5
Responses to Questions Dealing with Experiences with and Attitudes Toward Parole Officers and Parole Officer Aides by Parolees

	1973 Respondents				1974 Respondents			
	Parole Aides		Parole Officers		Parole Aides		Parole Officers	
	Number	%	Number	%	Number	%	Number	%
Can you communicate well with your parole officer?								
Yes	99	94.3	82	79.6	111	89.5	121	87.1
No	5	4.8	19	18.5	13	10.5	18	12.9
Do you trust your parole officer?								
Yes	87	82.9	79	76.7	95	77.9	111	81.6
No	17	16.2	20	19.4	27	22.1	25	18.4
Does he seem to care about what you say and do?								
Yes	100	95.2	90	87.4	112	94.9	125	91.2
No	5	4.8	8	7.8	6	5.1	12	8.8
Do other parolees assigned to your parole officer feel he is doing a good job?								
Yes	37	35.2	19	18.5	37	29.6	32	23.2
No	5	4.8	4	3.9	7	5.6	5	3.6
Don't know	61	58.1	78	75.7	81	64.8	101	73.2

Table 5-5 (cont.)

	1973 Respondents				1974 Respondents			
	Parole Aides		Parole Officers		Parole Aides		Parole Officers	
	Number	%	Number	%	Number	%	Number	%
How often do you "con" your parole officer?								
Often	4	3.8	5	4.9	8	7.8	11	10.3
Sometimes	21	20.0	23	22.3	29	28.4	15	14.0
Never	80	76.2	71	68.9	65	63.7	81	75.7
Would your parole officer do more for you than is required?								
Yes	79	75.2	71	68.9	77	70.0	98	76.6
No	14	13.3	19	18.5	33	30.0	30	23.4
Does your parole officer have connections he uses to help you get jobs?								
Yes	64	61.0	47	45.6	63	55.3	56	43.4
No	30	28.6	39	37.9	51	44.7	73	56.6
Does your parole officer understand what it is like to be on parole?								
Yes	83	79.0	60	58.3	103	84.4	83	66.4
No	15	14.3	30	29.1	19	15.6	42	33.6
Is your parole officer easy to find if you need to see him?								
Yes	97	92.4	88	85.4	104	83.9	128	92.8
No	7	6.7	13	12.6	20	16.1	10	7.2

How often do you have contact with your parole officer, in person or by telephone?								
More than once a week	17	16.2	5	4.9	8	6.5	4	2.9
Once a week	38	36.2	29	28.2	25	20.3	26	18.7
Twice a month	1	1.0	8	7.8	40	32.5	45	32.4
Less than twice a month	47	44.8	69	56.3	50	40.7	64	46.0
If you committed a parole violation, would your parole officer give you a second chance?								
Yes	37	35.2	35	34.0	37	30.1	47	33.8
No	2	1.9	5	4.9	9	7.3	7	5.0
Don't know	66	62.9	63	61.2	77	62.6	85	61.2
Are you required to visit your parole officer at his office, or does he visit you at home or on the job?								
Visit required at office	35	33.3	19	18.5	38	31.4	42	31.8
Officer visits parolee	52	49.5	74	71.9	72	59.5	81	61.4
Both	15	14.3	9	8.7	11	9.1	9	6.8

contact whoever is supervising them on parole is important if the whole concept of parole is to be viable. Nevertheless, it is to be expected that aides' parolees could get in touch with them much more easily than could parolees supervised by a parole officer. One major reason for this is that aides have only one-half the number of parolees to supervise than does the typical parole officer. However, parolees contacted in 1974 indicated that parole officers were easier to find than aides. This seems again to indicate a different type of aide employed the second year from the first. Because of the difference in caseloads, one would also expect that parolees assigned to aides would have more contact with them than parolees assigned to parole officers. This is what Table 5-5 indicates. Parolees supervised by an aide report more contacts and meetings than parolees supervised by regular parole officers. Parolees supervised by those aides who started during the first year of the program report considerably more contacts with their aide than those supervised by the new aides.

There is little difference in the two groups of parolees' evaluation of whether their aide or officer would give them a second chance if they were discovered committing a parole violation.

Parolees were asked to rank their parole officers or aides on the same four scales utilized earlier by field workers and unit supervisors in ranking these employees (see Table 5-6). Parolees rated aides superior to parole officers on all four scales in 1973; however in 1974, parolees rated parole officers on the average to be consistently superior. Supervisors had ranked parole officers superior to parole officer aides both years.

The first three scales attempt to measure characteristics that many parole officers and supervisors had indicated to the evaluation staff were most important in differentiating between good and average parole officers. Assuming the scores to be additive, supervisors rated parole officers somewhat superior to aides in 1973 (223 compared with 219) and more so in 1974 (213 compared to

Table 5-6
Parolees' Ranking of Parole Officer Aides and Parole Officers on Several Indicators (Rated on scale from 0 = poor to 100 = excellent)

	1973 Respondents		1974 Respondents	
	Parole Aides	Parole Officers	Parole Aides	Parole Officers
	$\overline{X}$	$\overline{X}$	$\overline{X}$	$\overline{X}$
Ability to motivate parolees	76.2	73.3	76.7	76.7
Ability to relate to parolees	79.1	76.8	79.2	81.1
Willingness to put himself out	78.4	75.9	72.3	78.0
Overall quality of performance as a parole officer	80.7	78.8	78.1	83.4

199). Parolees rated parole officers considerably lower than aides in 1973 when the three scale scores are combined (226 compared with 234), but higher in 1974 (236 compared with 228). However, when parole officer aides hired during the first year of the program are compared with parole officers in 1974, supervisors and parolees consistently rank the aides as equally competent. Parole officer aides with a year's experience were rated higher than parole officers by parolees on every scale and question designed to measure effectiveness. However, when all aides are compared to parole officers, the officers are ranked higher by parolees in 1974 inasmuch as the new aides pull the overall aides' average effectiveness down considerably. The first year's evaluation concluded that aides may be rated more effective by parolees because of their similarity to parolees, i.e., also being ex-offenders. At least one other possible explanation for these differences may be the variation in aides' and officers' size of caseloads, which affects the time allocation per case. Several studies have concluded that the more contact time prisoners, parolees, welfare recipients, and others have with social-service personnel, the more satisfied they are with the service they receive.[1] This feeling of satisfaction appears to be an artifact of the contact time,[2] inasmuch as external changes in behavior have not necessarily been associated with these feelings.[3]

Therefore, those parolees supervised by aides who feel they are receiving better supervision may think so because the aides have more time to spend with them than does the average parole officer. Whether contact time is responsible for at least part of the favorable evaluation aides received from parolees in 1973 is impossible to discern; however, it does not appear to be as relevant as other variables in light of the 1974 evaluation.

If aides are equally as good at helping parolees or better than parole officers, one could expect aides' parolees to have had fewer legal problems since their release from prison. In order to ascertain this, parolees were asked four questions concerning their legal problems since parole. The questions dealt with whether they had been questioned by the police since their release from prison, arrested, arraigned, or reincarcerated during this time. Parolees' responses are given in Table 5-7.

The parolees working with aides have had considerably more legal problems since their release from prison. Since their release from prison they have been questioned more by the police, arrested more frequently, arraigned more often in court on more new offenses, and also been reincarcerated or jailed more often. If one were to evaluate the effectiveness of parole officers in comparison to aides on the basis of their clients' legal problems (assuming the two groups of clients are similar), one would have to conclude that parole officers are far superior to aides. However, the caseloads of aides and parole officers are considerably different. Aides' parolees were incarcerated longer for more serious offenses, have more extensive past criminal histories, and were on the average younger when first arrested (see Table 3-4). The aides' parolees, in other words,

Table 5-7
Responses by Parolees to Questions Dealing with Legal Contacts Since Release from Prison

| | 1973 Respondents | | | | 1974 Respondents | | | |
| | Parole Aides | | Parole Officers | | Parole Aides | | Parole Officers | |
	Number	%	Number	%	Number	%	Number	%
Have the police questioned you about any crime since your release from prison?								
Yes	24	22.9	23	22.3	39	31.5	33	23.9
No	80	76.2	78	75.7	85	68.5	105	76.1
Have the police arrested you since your release from prison?								
Yes	38	36.2	31	30.1	43	34.7	47	33.8
No	105	62.9	103	68.9	81	65.3	92	66.2
Have you been to court for a new offense (except traffic) since your release from prison?								
Yes	25	23.8	15	14.6	27	21.8	29	20.9
No	79	75.2	88	85.4	97	78.2	110	79.1
Have you spent time in jail since your release from prison?								
Yes	32	30.5	28	27.2	38	30.6	33	23.9
No	72	68.6	75	72.8	86	69.4	105	76.1

have the characteristics of those most likely to recidivate. In fact, if one controls for prior criminal involvement and age at first arrest, *aides' parolees have slightly lower rates of legal problems* than parole officers' parolees.

The 1973 evaluation of the Parole Officer Aide Program concluded that aides were rated as superior to parole officers by parolees on every indicator. It is apparent from the 1974 data that being an ex-offender parole officer is certainly no guarantee of receiving a positive evaluation from a parolee. The additional ex-offenders hired the second year of the program were not as carefully selected, and their performance has generally not been rated as satisfactorily as those employed the first year by parolees, supervisors, and field workers or as predicted from attitudinal indices. The data from both years, however, reflect more similarities between parole officer aides and parole officers than possible differences. The recent data certainly indicate the importance of screening potential employees, whether they be ex-offenders or not.

Summary

Responses to interviews and questionnaires by parole supervisors, prison inmates, and parolees reflect general agreement that the Parole Officer Aide Program is worthwhile. Supervisors ranked parole officer aides higher than parole officers only on effort and ability to get parolees jobs, yet they saw aides as a valuable source of information for parole officers and as teachers for parole officers on how to relate to parolees. Inmates consistently indicated a preference for parole officer aides, with more than two-thirds of them expressing a desire to be employed as an aide. Parolees supervised by aides consistently ranked them high on all scales. The researchers suggest this might be due to the smaller caseloads of parole officer aides, which allow them to devote more time to each of their parolees, but this does not appear to be the only justification in light of the 1974 data. The final portion of the parolee questionnaire indicates that parolees under an aide's supervision consistently had more legal problems. This is apparently the result of aides being assigned parolees who are more likely to be "losers" rather than parole officers aides providing inferior service to their parolees.

National Survey of States' Use
of Ex-Offenders in Parole and
Probation Work

As is evident from the previous chapters, there has been a rapid increase and interest in using paraprofessionals in the helping services, especially during the last decade. Consequently, the literature on the use of paraprofessionals has become much more common. All reports indicate that paraprofessionals are being utilized not only more extensively, but in ever-widening areas. The current information also suggests that most programs have been declared more or less successful. As the research results concerning the use of paraprofessionals have become more widely known, the criminal justice agencies have more diligently explored the possible use of indigenous workers in correctional programs. The Joint Commission on Correctional Manpower and Training has expressly encouraged correctional agencies to hire ex-offenders to mitigate their manpower shortages.[1] As recently as 1973 the National Advisory Commission on Criminal Justice Standards and Goals urged correctional agencies to actively hire ex-offenders to assist in working with convicted offenders.[2]

While the literature has indicated widespread use of ex-offender employees in corrections, many practitioners have claimed that the self-help movement in the area of corrections is more rhetorical than operable.[3] The actual number and types of programs being used by various state correctional agencies have not been compiled in recent years. The last reported statistics were compiled by The National Council on Crime and Delinquency in 1967 and are summarized in Chapter 1 (see Tables 1-1, 1-2, 1-3). The lack of such data appears to have been an inhibiting factor for some states to implement such programs. One state director of corrections recently commented: "We hear all the time about the great potential of ex-offender programs for corrections, but we never see any data on who's using them and what the results are."

As part of the Parole Officer Aide evaluation, an attempt has been made to compile a current and complete survey of the types and numbers of indigenous paraprofessional (ex-offender) programs being used in the nation, especially in the areas of probation and parole. This chapter reports the findings of that survey.

The Survey

The survey of the use of ex-offenders in corrections began in March, 1974. A twenty-two-item questionnaire, with a covering letter explaining the purpose of the survey, was sent to the administrative head of the Department of Corrections in each state. The purpose of the survey was to ascertain some baseline data as to the use of ex-offender paraprofessionals, as well as various attitudes toward the use of such indigenous workers. Every two weeks follow-up mailings were sent to every nonrespondent—in some cases as many as five follow-up letters were sent. Within twelve weeks, mailed responses had been received from forty-eight of the fifty-one polled administrators. The remaining three state directors were interviewed by telephone.

One major problem became apparent as the questionnaires were returned. Since the questionnaire contained items concerned with parole and probation, as well as a general category labeled "other," referring to work done by ex-offenders in corrections outside of the probation and parole system, many states duplicated the questionnaire received by the director of corrections and circulated it to other agencies. Thus, multiple responses were received from seven states, reflecting, for example, the perspectives of directors of halfway houses and youth commissions. The record for cooperation in this regard belongs to New Jersey, from which ten completed questionnaires were received. Therefore, on questions dealing with parole and probation, the decision was made to report only the responses received from the various state directors of corrections, unless the state director of probation was the principal respondent. The multiple responses from the various states are reflected for the most part only in the general category of "other." The multiple answers that were received were simply averaged together to assign an overall response from that state.

One other serious limitation of the data is reflected in the fact that several states do not have a centralized probation service. In California, for example, probation is strictly a county function (with the exception of the state probation subsidy program), while in Ohio, one-half of the counties are supervised by the state central office while the other half remain autonomous. Apparently, in several of the states with decentralized probation programs, no one knows the entirety of what is going on throughout the state in the field of probation. The emphasis in this report will therefore be on the use of ex-offenders as parole officers or aides.

The Use of Ex-Offenders

It was unquestionably difficult for many state directors of corrections to respond accurately to whether their state used ex-offenders as parole or probation officers or aides. One of the major reasons for this difficulty was simply that in at least nine states there are no legal or administrative restrictions against ex-offenders in state employment. Consequently, little effort is made to document whether correctional employees have criminal records or not, several directors maintained. Typical comments from these states were similar to these from Oregon:

The Corrections Division has no specific program to hire former offenders, and certainly no specific funding for that purpose. Conversely, we have no bias against hiring any individual whose background and ability qualify him or her for a specific position.

The respondent went on to say that following his canvass of personnel officers serving various units of the Corrections Division, several employees were identified as former offenders.

Sixteen, or approximately one-third, of the states reported the use of ex-offenders as parole officers or aides (see Table 6-1). The number of such employees range from one such employee in five states to twenty-three in Ohio, and fifty-five ex-offender employees in Pennsylvania (see Table 6-2).

Using former offenders as parole officers is a relatively new phenomenon, as judged by the initial dates given for the initiation of such practices (see Table 6-3). California began its program in 1967; Washington in 1968; and four states,

Table 6-1
State Responses to the Use of Ex-Offenders in Corrections

Category	States Using Ex-Offenders	(Percent)	States Not Using Ex-Offenders	(Percent)
Parole officer aide	16	34.0	31	66.0
Probation officer aide	10	24.4	31	75.6
Other[a]	22[a]	100.0	0	0.0

[a]Includes correctional officers, teachers, work-release directors, community volunteers, halfway-house counselors, other professional positions, business office personnel, work-release supervisors, program coordinators, clerical support in probation and parole services, teachers' aides, probation officers, cooks and related service workers, research assistants, engineers, other institutional jobs not involving custody, treatment aides in drug programs, advocates, cottage parents, and employment counselors.

Table 6-2
Number of Ex-Offenders Actually Employed by Number of States

Type Employment	1	2-5	6-10	11-15	16-30	31-60	Total
Parole	5[a]	1	5	2	1	1	139
Probation	1[a]	1	2	2	0	0	41
Other	0	5	2	3	3	1	203

[a]Several states failed to report the number of ex-offender parole or probation officer aides they employed—thus, the total in row one is only 15 states.

Table 6-3
Year in Which State Program Using Ex-Offenders Began

Category	Date	States	Percent
Parole	1967	1	6.3
	1968	1	6.3
	1969	0	0.0
	1970	4	25.0
	1971	4	25.0
	1972	5	31.3
	1973	1	6.3
		16	100.0
Probation	1968	1	12.5
	1969	0	0.0
	1970	4	50.0
	1971	1	12.5
	1972	2	25.0
		8[a]	100.0
Others	Early 50s	1	5.3
	1969	2	10.5
	1970	3	15.8
	1971	3	15.8
	1972	6	31.6
	1973	4	21.1
		19[a]	100.0

[a]Three states failed to report when their parole or probation officer aide program began. The N under others represents programs rather than states.

Alaska, Maryland, Utah, and Wisconsin, report similar programs beginning in 1970. In 1971, four additional states initiated ex-offender parole officer programs; five more states implemented such programs in 1972; and one state reported beginning a program in 1973. Apparently 1970-72 was the period when most of these programs began. In fact, of the 139 ex-offender parole officer aides presently employed throughout the United States, 117, or over 84 percent, are employed in states that initiated their programs during this period. It may be of interest to note that all thirteen programs that began between 1970 and 1972 received LEAA funding. Of the ex-offender parole officer aide programs initiated before this time, only one of the three reported federal funding. The tremendous growth and adoption of such programs may, therefore, be an outgrowth of federal interests in supporting such innovations.

The use of probation officer aides has followed a similar line of development and funding as parole officer aides. All but one of the state programs, begun since 1970, received federal funding. Of particular note is the fact that all ten states with probation officer aide programs also have parole officer aide programs.

States' Legal and Administrative Restrictions Concerning Employing Ex-Offenders

Several state directors mentioned that one of the motivating factors for initiating their ex-offender parole officer aide program was the need to set an example for other employers to hire ex-offenders. A typical comment was: "The commission cannot ask other employers to consider hiring ex-offenders without first hiring them ourselves." Despite the validity of such logic, administrative or legal restrictions limit the employment of ex-offenders for parole or probation work in fifteen states.[4] Eleven state directors of correction report legal restrictions such as the following:

1. Parole officers are "peace officers" and must be licensed to carry firearms, and it is against our state law for a convicted felon to carry a firearm.

2. The state, county, or municipality may not employ a person convicted of a felony who has not, prior to the time of filing an employment application, received a full pardon.

3. Our state personnel still refuses to hire if a potential employee has been convicted of a felony or is under felony indictment.

4. Convicted felons lose their citizenship and cannot be sworn to oath of office until citizenship is restored.

5. Convicted felons cannot by law be appointed to a position of trust.

Nine states reported administrative restrictions limiting the employment of ex-offenders in parole or probation work. In four of these nine states there were no legal restrictions, only administrative ones. Typical restrictions reported were:

1. Our policy is that an applicant with a criminal record must have received a pardon for each convicted offense before employment is considered.

2. It is simply not done in our state. We want employees we can trust and you never know about ex-cons.

3. The use of ex-offenders as parole or probation officer aides does not have the support of experienced probation and parole officer personnel but appears to be limited mostly to academic theorists. The role of the ex-offender must be limited, and he should never be allowed to exercise any of the supervisory control over offenders.

In addition to legal and administrative restrictions prohibiting ex-offenders' employment in parole and probation work, other factors discourage many ex-offenders from participating in such programs. Low monetary compensation is no doubt one determining factor. The average beginning pay for such employees is $483.52 per month, or $5802.21 per year. The highest beginning pay for parole or probation aides is in Alaska, where the minimal starting pay is $687.00 per month, or $8244.00 per year. The pay scale for ex-offenders in parole or probation work is also quite limited. Often aides are unable to advance to higher professional levels, and therefore, their maximal earnings are considerably restricted. The maximal salaries for ex-offender aides range from $6684 to $16,800 per year with the average maximal salary being $10,352, or $862.67 per month. With such financial barriers and the additional administrative and professional restrictions, aides in some positions may be locked into a low-paying job with little hope of advancement within the agency.

While definite barriers exist in some states, several state and federal agencies actively recruit ex-offenders for their respective parole and probation aide programs, as well as other important positions. For example, several state ombudsmen were formerly ex-offender parole officer aides. At least one assistant prison warden was a former aide, and one administrative assistant to a state director of correctional services is a former offender. Thus, in some instances the former offender who selects a career in criminal justice can progress professionally and receive better compensations.

Another positive point of the ex-offender parole and probation programs is the opportunity provided aides for educational advancement. Twelve of the sixteen states that utilize ex-offenders as parole or probation officer aides provide paid release time from the job for educational advancement. In addition, financial aid is available in at least eleven of the sixteen states to defray the educational expenses. Such available support and encouragement may solve the dilemma of low pay by preparing the former offender aides for better-paying jobs.

Criteria Used in Selecting Ex-Offenders for Employment in Correctional Work

Selection of paraprofessionals remains an apparent problem for most helping agencies. Twenty-eight state directors of corrections requested the researchers provide them a list of criteria on how other states select ex-offender aides. One director of corrections commented:

One of the reasons our state has been reluctant to start programs using ex-offenders as parole or probation officers is our uncertainty as to how reliable, dependable and trustworthy ex-cons can be identified. Certainly, public opinion is not apt to be highly mobilized if ex-offenders as correctional personnel were to become involved in legal problems.

Many directors of corrections appear to be somewhat reluctant to accept such new programs without definite guidelines on how ex-offender aides should be selected, and how they are being selected in other states.

It is clearly evident from the survey that a definite lack of consensus exists among the various states in selecting aides (see Table 6-4). The criterion for employment most frequently mentioned was the ability of the ex-offender to articulate and communicate with others. Other criteria frequently mentioned were good adjustment on the part of the ex-offender during and after parole, presently free of correctional supervision, and a set minimum educational achievement level. (This varied from eighth grade in one state to a college degree in another.) Several directors mentioned that although criteria were established for selecting ex-offender aides, often these were ignored or overlooked if a particularly good prospect were being considered.

Job Performance of Ex-Offender Aides

The major question of all ex-offender programs concerns their successfulness. State directors of correction were asked to rank (on a scale from 0 to 100, with 50 being average) the overall job performance of their ex-offender aides in comparison to regular staff members performing similar tasks. Overall, aides' performance was rated very good for the sixteen states, the average being 67.8, with a range from 30 to 100. Aides are apparently judged to be highly effective in those states where they are employed.

Table 6-4
Criteria Used in Selection of Ex-Offenders for Employment in Corrections by State

Criteria	States
Ability to communicate	5
Adjustment during and/or after parole supervision	4[a]
Presently free of correctional supervision	4
Certain educational minimum achievement	4
Other[b]	10

[a]The number is greater than 15 because most states mentioned more than one criterion.

[b]Includes: Stability, maturity, reliability, honesty, potential, integrity, interest, no discernible situational problems, at least average intelligence, enthusiasm, good behavior while incarcerated, successful completion of extended training program while incarcerated, dependability, freedom from sexual deviancy, and willingness and ability to participate in college program, plus same criteria as for any other potential employees.

Certainly if the field of corrections is to utilize the ex-offender in a meaningful role, the support of correctional personnel is essential. The Joint Commission on Correctional Manpower's 1967 survey found that over 50 percent of the correctional personnel interviewed felt it would not be a good idea to hire ex-offenders in their agency.[5] The current survey found a definite shift in this respect. Eighty percent of the state directors felt it desirable to hire ex-offenders in their agencies today. Moreover, in those states utilizing ex-offenders as aides, directors were even more complimentary and committed to the idea than in states not using such programs. Although the desirability of such programs between states utilizing and not utilizing ex-offenders are not statistically significantly different, there does appear to be less opposition to such new programs today, even in those states that have not implemented them.

All state directors of correction were asked to list both the advantages and disadvantages of utilizing ex-offenders as parole or probation officers or aides. The advantages most often mentioned were the greater rapport ex-offenders were able to develop with parolees and probationers, and the ability of the ex-offenders to empathize with the problems experienced by the parolees and probationers (see Table 6-5). Several directors made such comments as: "They [the offenders] bring with them the unique quality of being on both sides of the correctional process and thereby can more readily identify with offenders' fears and problems." Another typical comment was:

It gives some legitimacy to our requesting employers to consider hiring an ex-offender if we have some on our own staff. It's pretty difficult justifying to a potential employer why he should hire an ex-con if your own agency refuses to hire them.

One final advantage mentioned by a number of directors dealt with the mediating role such employees could perform between parolees and the parole department.

They [ex-offenders] could teach us how parolees think and why they do some of the "crazy" things they do. In addition, they could justify many of our policies and rules to parolees in a way that they might accept them. Hell, we can use any help nowadays that we can get regardless of the source.

The major disadvantages mentioned by state directors of corrections in utilizing ex-offender employees center around negative stereotypes former offenders still reflect (see Table 6-6). Comments by directors included: "[The professional staff] would be incensed by lowering our selection criteria." "Public support can certainly not be counted on if your office is packed with ex-offenders." "Hiring such undesirables is simply inviting the corruption of your office and clients." Such reactions tend to support Geis's earlier observation that self-righteousness lies at the core of the public contempt for offenders.[6] Certainly public opinion can be mobilized, placated, and won over.

Table 6-5
Major Advantages Cited by States for Employing Ex-Offender Parole/Probation Officer Aides[a]

Advantages	Number of States
Greater rapport with clients	33
Better understanding of client's problems	19
More capable of empathizing	14
Streetwise	9
Additional line of communication to the community	9
Resource and mediator	8
Unique support for professional staff	6
Stronger commitment to the job	5
Additional source of manpower	4
Other[b]	13
None	5
Total	125

[a]Frequency of responses does not add to 50, because some states gave several advantages.

[b]Includes: affirmative action, opportunity for ex-offender to contribute to criminal justice field and perform public relations services, better ability to avoid being "conned," reality-based approach to offenders from a staff position, ability to enter areas where officers would fear to tread.

In the case of the ex-offender this may be done most efficiently by appeals to the public's self-interest (demonstration of the effectiveness of ex-offenders in working with parolees curbing crime), combined with the reiterated support of societal standards (i.e., everyone should have an equal opportunity to compete). A major deficiency of ex-offenders gaining such public support is their lack of a major spokesman. Without such vocal support, negative public opinion continues and ex-offenders tend to operate from a weak and most vulnerable position.

The 1974 survey of the fifty states and the District of Columbia found considerably more support for using ex-offenders in correctional work than was the case in 1967. Not only did more states favor using such indigenous workers in 1974, but several states had implemented such programs since 1967. Most of the programs implemented since 1967 were supported by federal funding. Whether the states are truly committed to the idea of utilizing ex-offender personnel may be more accurately answered when such federal funding is no longer available.

It does appear that the ex-offender's involvement in corrections may continue to increase, if for no other reason than the phenomenon of "jumping on the bandwagon." Using ex-offenders as parole or probation officers and aides is a relatively new idea. Given the criticism corrections has recently received, adopting new programs in this area may at least dissipate some of this criticism. However, state directors of corrections where ex-offenders are presently being utilized as probation or parole officers or aides appear much more committed to the desirability of such programs than directors in states where such programs are not in use (see Table 6-7). Whether or not utilizing ex-offenders in corrections affects state directors' attitudes favorably, or whether directors already favoring such programs are the ones implementing them, cannot be answered from these data. It is very apparent, however, that utilizing ex-offenders as parole or probation officer aides is considered very desirable today by most state directors of corrections.

The future role of ex-offenders in correctional work may well be determined by top administrators in the respective state correctional departments. Unless such programs are supported by those in decision-making positions, it is unlikely

Table 6-6
Major Disadvantages Cited by States for Not Employing Ex-Offender Parole/Probation Officer Aides[a]

Disadvantages	Number of States
Professional staff's resistance	16
Possible adverse publicity	12
Possibility of them corrupting their parolees or probationers	12
Difficulty of finding suitable candidates	10
Overidentification with client	4
Lack of career ladder	3
Expense in resocializing and training	3
Lack of information and experience in running such programs	2
Lack of most ex-cons, in education and intelligence	2
None	4
Other[b]	13
Total	81

[a]Frequency of responses does not add to 50, because some states gave several disadvantages.

[b]Includes: generally assigned only menial tasks, possible rabble-rousing for no effective purpose, lack of effectiveness except in drug treatment programs, nonacceptance by clients, too much expected from sole factor of ex-offender status, inability to deal with strengths and weaknesses of the system, protection of confidentiality of records, high turnover rate, inclination to disregard official policy, police resistance, and undependable ability.

that they will survive for long. This factor alone supports the relevancy of the national survey conducted and reported by the research staff.

A summary of the various states' responses to the 1974 survey is provided in Table 6-8. Judging from the survey, there appears to be growing and continuing support for implementing ex-offender programs on a wider basis. Their success or failure may be determined not only by the quality of ex-offenders selected, but also by the support such programs receive from professionals in the field. If professionals accept ex-offenders as complementary co-workers, as they apparently have in Ohio, the ex-offender programs are much more likely to be successful. On the other hand, if the professional staff view such new employees as threatening their own positions and compromising the dignity and respect of their agency, such programs will certainly fail.

The use of ex-offenders in corrections is a unique and refreshing approach. Not only does it convey the trust of the state in hiring ex-offenders for responsible positions, but it indicates the willingness of the state to seek new ways to help ex-offenders. Both of these goals are certainly laudable. The growth and acceptance of such programs during the last seven years has been remarkable. If the growth and acceptance of such programs continues at the present rate, ex-offender parole officers and aides will be a common and important part of the correctional helping team of the future.

Summary

One part of the evaluation of the Parole Officer Aide Program consisted of compiling a current and complete survey of the ex-offender programs being used throughout the United States, especially in the areas of probation and parole. A twenty-two-item questionnaire was sent to the administrative head of the Department of Corrections in each state and the District of Columbia.

Table 6-7
Desirability of State's Utilizing Ex-Offenders as Parole or Probation Officer Aides

States	Desirability			
	Undesirable	Desirable	Very Desirable	Total
Utilizing ex-offender officers	2 (12.5%)	9 (56.2%)	5 (31.3%)	16
Not utilizing ex-offender officers	7 (25.9%)	17 (63.0%)	3 (11.1%)	27
Total	9 (20.9%)	26 (60.5%)	8 (18.6%)	43

Table 6-8

The Use of Ex-Offenders in Parole and Probation Work as Reported by State Directors of Corrections

	Utilize Ex-Offender Parole/Probation Officer Aide	Ex-Offenders Employed in "Other" Correctional Positions	Legal Restrictions Exist	Administrative Restrictions Exist	Desirability of Ex-Offender Programs	Released Time for Education	Financial Aid for Education	Number of Ex-Offenders Employed as Parole/Probation Aides
Alabama	X		X		U			
Alaska	X	X			D	X	X	12
Arizona		X			D			
Arkansas					D			
California	X	X		X	D	X		10
Colorado		X			D			
Connecticut		X			U	X	X	
Delaware					VD			
District of Columbia		X		X	VD	X	X	
Florida	X	X			D	X	X	11
Georgia		X						
Hawaii				X	D			
Idaho	X	X	X		U	X	X	1
Illinois	X				VD	X	X	9
Indiana		X			D			
Iowa	X	X			VD	X	X	1
Kansas					D			

State							
Kentucky	X			VD		X	4
Louisiana	X						
Maine				D			
Maryland	X[a]	X	X	D	X[a]	X[a]	
Massachusetts	X		X	VD			
Michigan	X			D			1
Minnesota	X					X	
Mississippi				U			
Missouri	X			VD	X		
Montana							
Nebraska				D			
Nevada				U			
New Hampshire				U			
New Jersey	X	X		D/VD	X	X	7
New Mexico				D			
New York		X	X	D			
North Carolina		X		D	X	X	
North Dakota		X		D			
Ohio	X	X	X	VD	X	X	23
Oklahoma		X		D			
Oregon							
Pennsylvania	X			D	X	X	55
Rhode Island				D			
South Carolina				U			
South Dakota				D			
Tennessee		X		D			
Texas			X				

Table 6-8 (cont.)

	Utilize Ex-Offender Parole/Probation Officer Aide	Ex-Offenders Employed in "Other" Correctional Positions	Legal Restrictions Exist	Administrative Restrictions Exist	Desirability of Ex-Offender Programs	Released Time for Education	Financial Aid for Education	Number of Ex-Offenders Employed as Parole/Probation Aides
Utah	X				D	X	X	2
Vermont	X				D	X	X	
Virginia	X	X			D			1
Washington	X				U	X	X	11
West Virginia		X						
Wisconsin	X	X			D	X		
Wyoming			X	X	U			
Total	16	22	11	9	--	17	16	
Percent	31.4	43.1	21.6	17.6	--	33.3	31.4	

aDiscontinued in 1972. Total does not include this program.

Sixteen states reported the use of ex-offenders as parole officers or aides. This practice seemed to be a fairly recent innovation, with 1970-72 being the period in which most of these programs began. One of the factors for initiating the ex-offender parole officer aide program seems to have been the need to set an example for other employers to hire ex-offenders.

Several factors inhibit ex-offenders from participating in such correctional programs. Some of these are legal and administrative restrictions, low monetary compensation, and little or no opportunity for advancement to a higher professional level. However, many of the ex-offender programs provide paid release time from the job for educational advancement. Such support may enable the ex-offender to obtain a better job.

State directors of correction rated the aides' performance as being very good, and 80 percent of the directors felt that it was desirable to hire ex-offenders in their agencies today. Thus, it seems that the use of ex-offender programs will continue to be supported and expanded.

7 Conclusions

This concluding chapter attempts to give a concise overview of the Ohio Parole Officer Aide Program and the various approaches utilized by the research staff of the Program for the Study of Crime and Delinquency in its evaluation. In addition, several recommendations and implications for using ex-offenders as paraprofessionals in the field of corrections are offered for consideration.

Background on the Project

The use of ex-offenders to aid and assist with probationers or parolees in the Department of Corrections is not original with Ohio. Several other states have utilized ex-offenders in one capacity or another in correctional programs. Two things about the Ohio Parole Officer Aide Program are relatively novel, however. First, the authority, power, and trust given ex-offenders who are hired as aides is unique. Although the aides do not have the total autonomy of parole officers, they do have their own caseloads, for which they are primarily responsible. Second, the desire and commitment of the Ohio Adult Parole Authority to objectively evaluate the effectiveness of the program is exceptional, and definitely commendable. In these and other respects, the Ohio Adult Parole Authority is capitalizing on the resources of ex-offenders and evaluating their effectiveness more extensively than have other states.

Summary of the Evaluation

In evaluating the twenty-three parole officer aides employed by the State of Ohio during the past two years, their performance in comparison to a control group of parole officers has been found equally effective. As a result, the Ohio Adult Parole Authority is in the process of hiring additional aides and broadening their responsibilities.

The research techniques employed in evaluating the effectiveness of the parole officer aides included a variety of approaches. The first technique utilized was the measurement of aides' and parole officers' attitudes on several dimensions associated with successful social-service workers. The results indicate that aides do have the qualities, attitudes, and orientations generally associated with successful social service workers. More similarities than differences were found between aides and parole officers on these various attitudinal indicators as well as in their attitudes toward law and order.

The in-depth interviews with parole officer aides indicate that they are very pleased with their jobs. They have been well accepted and socialized into their respective parole offices. Aides had considerable confidence in their own ability to help and assist parolees, although only four felt that being an ex-offender was more important than being a community resident in working with parolees.

The third approach followed in evaluating the program was the use of students as field observers. The students reported no difference in the number of parolees seen on the average by the various parole officers and parole officer aides. Similarly, no differences were observed in the percentage of time spent with parolees. Also, parole officers and parole officer aides' relationships with fellow workers were rated equal, but aides were evaluated as having somewhat better relations with their parolees than parole officers.

Unit supervisors rated parole officers and aides on several indicators as a fourth technique in evaluating the program. Their ratings indicate that in most respects parole officers are superior to aides. Supervisors in 1973 rated parole officer aides better in getting parolees jobs and "putting themselves out." However, in 1974, supervisors rated parole officers superior on every indicator. This is apparently a reflection of the type of aides hired during the second year of the program. In comparing supervisors' ratings of aides according to length of employment, those hired during the first year of the program in comparison to the second were rated higher on every dimension. In fact, if supervisors' ratings for parole officer aides hired during the 1972-73 program year are compared to parole officers, there is very little difference between the two groups. Aides are rated somewhat better in relating, helping, and getting parolees jobs, while parole officers are rated higher in motivating parolees and considerably better at report writing. Overall, however, supervisors in whose units aides worked were very excited about the Parole Officer Aide Program. Several supervisors indicated that they had grave doubts about the program at its inception, but they now felt that it was the best new program to have ever come out of the Adult Parole Authority, and that it should certainly be expanded.

The fifth indicator in assessing the desirability of the ex-offender program was to ascertain inmates' attitudes toward such an innovation. Inmates surveyed at Ohio's penal institutions were very much in favor of the Parole Officer Aide Program. The majority of inmates felt that parolees supervised by an aide would be more likely to succeed on parole. An overwhelming majority of inmates indicated that they would prefer being supervised by an aide rather than a parole officer. Surprisingly, although the program has been in effect for two years, fewer than 50 percent of the inmates were aware of the program.

A sixth approach used in the evaluation was to ask the parolees supervised by parole officers and parole officer aides their opinions of the help and support they were receiving. The parolees surveyed, who were under the supervision of either an aide or a parole officer, rated parole officer aides superior on every indicator in 1973, and rated parole officers somewhat better than parole officer aides in 1974. Parole officer aides in 1973 were rated more trustworthy, more concerned, more helpful in finding jobs, more understanding, easier to talk with, and easier to find when needed by parolees than were parole officers. Such was not the case in 1974, when all parole officer aides were simply compared to the control group of parole officers.

The reason for such differing results seems to lie with the type of parole officer aide hired during the first and the second year of the program. The 1973 program evaluation mentioned that the aides' smaller caseload might be responsible for the most positive ratings parole officer aides received from parolees. This explanation now seems somewhat less accurate. A more realistic explanation may simply be that aides, carefully chosen, can be a real asset to an Adult Parole Authority's service. However, being an ex-offender is no guarantee that an individual will make a good parole officer or aide. Consequently, screening of applicants should be followed in order to insure the program's success.

A seventh approach in assessing the ex-offender program was a national survey of State Directors of Corrections. This survey documented the growing trend of utilizing ex-offenders in corrections as support personnel. The majority of directors favored using ex-offenders as parole officers or aides, but only Ohio and Pennsylvania have actually implemented programs where a sizable number of such ex-offenders are employed.

Recommendations

From our work and contact with the Ohio Parole Officer Aide Program during the last two years, we have received information from numerous sources concerning recommended changes. It is from such suggestions as well as the evaluation of the data collected that the following recommendations are made:

Selection of Parole Officer Aides

Greater care should be given in selecting ex-offenders as parole officer aides. On the basis of this evaluation, an aide's effectiveness can be predicted from various attitudinal scales and indices associated with successful social service type workers. The Adult Parole Authority should consider having applicants screened on the basis of their scores on tests such as the achievement motivation scale, self-esteem score, focal concerns scale, and the dogmatism scale.

Training Seminars

All new aides should attend an orientation and training seminar. Such seminars should emphasize skills such as report writing, dictating, and counseling techniques. The training seminar should be conducted in such a way that the parole officer aides will be enthusiastic about their jobs.

Retraining Seminars

All parole officer aides should be invited to participate in at least part of each new training seminar. This will allow aides to share experiences as well as receive a refresher course in parole techniques. This will also help aides to get to know one another, and perhaps provide the additional support and advice needed. In addition, aides will be able to learn from one another how they have dealt with precarious situations.

Relations with Police and
Jail Personnel

Police and jail personnel in cities where aides will work should be invited to a portion of the training seminar. Their understanding of the program should facilitate aides in gaining the needed cooperation from local law-enforcement agencies. If such police and jail officials do not attend the training seminar, correspondence from the Parole Officer Aide Project Director explaining the program and requesting their assistance would be helpful. Literature describing the program and its success should be made available not only to these agencies but to others with which the parole officer aides will be working.

Assignment of Aides to
Parole Units

A conscientious effort should be made to assign aides to communities with which they are acquainted. This will allow aides to more fully utilize their knowledge of the community and its resources in working with parolees. From interviews, the parole officer aides indicate that knowledge of the community is more important to them in helping parolees than is their status of being ex-offenders.

An Incentive Program and
Career Ladder

Aides should be provided an incentive to gain additional writing, speaking, and counseling skills. Such an incentive should be related with salary increments and advancement possibilities. As the aides gain the education and experience required for potential parole officer employees, they should be given *first* consideration for any new openings (an affirmative action type program). Such an incentive system would hold out viable, attainable goals for aides to work toward. Certainly the opportunity to become a parole officer and have the period of time when working as an aide count toward advancement, retirement, and other benefits is necessary.

Integration of Aides into
Parole Units

Unit supervisors should encourage an exchange of ideas and knowledge between aides and officers in their respective units. Aides may be of considerable help to parole officers in understanding parolees' problems, apprehensions, occupational desires and capabilities, and differences in "culture." Parole officers, on the other hand, may be of enormous help to parole officer aides in learning how best to cope with bureaucratic problems and workable solutions to various problems with parolees. The exchange can be most beneficial and complementary for the Adult Parole Authority.

Updating Training Seminars

At least two updating training seminars should be held each year for all parole officer aides. This would allow aides to receive additional training in areas in which they feel weak. It would also provide the means by which aides could communicate to each other various techniques which they find to be most successful in working with parolees, parole officers, and the Adult Parole Authority.

Public Relations and
Educational Programs

A more intensive and effective public information and education program should be conducted. The Adult Parole Authority should receive some recognition and praise for their innovative attempts in the field of corrections. Certainly, the parole officer aide program is one program the APA can take pride in. In addition, by informing the public of such programs, some of the resistance aides have encountered in their respective communities may be minimized.

Project Director's Duties

The parole officer aide's Project Director should allocate at least one-half and preferably all of his time to coordinate, implement, and monitor the project's programs and activities. This would allow for the preparation of training seminars and for the dissemination of relevant information concerning the program to the APA, regional and unit parole offices, parole officer aides, the press, and correctional departments in other states.

Evaluation of the Program

The parole officer aide program should be continuously evaluated by some outside agency. This will provide the Adult Parole Authority some baseline data to assess the effectiveness of the program. If the program is apparently less effective from one year to the next, the evaluation may supply some of the reasons. Similarly, since innovative ideas such as the parole officer aide program are more subject to ridicule and criticism by the press and the public, the sponsoring agency has a continuing responsibility to justify such programs with reliable empirical data.

Overall, Ohio's Parole Officer Aide Program has been given positive, often superlative, ratings from almost everyone associated with it. The aides have performed well in their two years of employment with the Ohio Adult Parole Authority. Regardless of whether parolees, supervisors, or others are evaluating their work, aides have received outstanding praise and acknowledgment for their contribution to the field of corrections.

Appendix

The Attitudinal Questionnaire

This study is being conducted by the Crime and Delinquency Research Center at The Ohio State University. We are conducting this survey to determine how people feel about trends in the area of corrections. We will be giving this questionnaire to various groups in the State of Ohio, and to some of these groups several times. Your cooperation on this survey will provide a better understanding of correctional staff's attitude and problems. No one will be allowed to see your answers except the Research Center staff.

This is not a test. There are no right or wrong answers. Your answers will be combined with all of the other respondents and be examined as a group. Your questionnaire will never be looked at individually. Please answer all of the questions to the best of your ability; and please be completely honest. You have the assurance of the directors of the Crime and Delinquency Research Center that no one in the correctional system will ever see your questionnaire and that you cannot possibly get into trouble as a result of your answers.

Thank you for your cooperation in this survey.

> Joseph E. Scott, Ph.D.
> Project Director

Instructions

The following statements are presented so that we can get an idea of how people feel about certain things. You should circle the response which best explains how you feel about the statement. We want to know how *you* feel about these things, not how you think someone else would answer or how someone would want you to answer. Remember that no one in the correctional system will ever see your answers and we want you to be completely honest in your response. Circle either strongly disagree, disagree, undecided, agree, or strongly agree; whichever answer you think best describes how you feel about the statement.

Here are a couple of examples of how you should circle the response you select.

A.   I like ice cream

Strongly Disagree	Disagree	Undecided	Agree	(Strongly Agree)

B.   The time of year I like best is winter.

Strongly Disagree	(Disagree)	Undecided	Agree	Strongly Agree

CARD I

Study number:

<u>Col. 1</u>
2

Card number:

<u>Col. 2</u>
1

Case number:

<u>Cols. 3-5</u>

Region office:

<u>Cols. 6-7</u>

Canton	00
Columbus	01
Akron	02
Youngstown	03
Cleveland	04
Cincinnati	05
Lima	06
Athens	07
Dayton	08
Toledo	09

From Enumeration Form:

1.   I like to do my best in whatever I undertake.

	Col. 8
Strongly disagree	1
Disagree	2
Undecided	3
Agree	4
Strongly agree	5
NA	9

2.   · Once people get to know me they usually don't like me.

	Col. 9
Strongly disagree	1
Disagree	2
Undecided	3
Agree	4
Strongly agree	5
NA	9

3.   I'd rather not have anyone telling me what to do.

	Col. 10
Strongly disagree	1
Disagree	2
Undecided	3
Agree	4
Strongly agree	5
NA	9

4.   I would like to do something that means a lot to other people.

	Col. 11
Strongly disagree	1
Disagree	2
Undecided	3
Agree	4
Strongly agree	5
NA	9

5.   I don't have too much respect for myself.

	Col. 12
Strongly disagree	1
Disagree	2
Undecided	3
Agree	4
Strongly agree	5
NA	9

6.   I never back down from a fight.

	Col. 13
Strongly disagree	1
Disagree	2
Undecided	3
Agree	4
Strongly agree	5
NA	9

7.   If somebody says I'm not good enough, I usually try harder.

	Col. 14
Strongly disagree	1
Disagree	2
Undecided	3
Agree	4
Strongly agree	5
NA	9

8. I think that most people like me.

	Col. 15
Strongly disagree	1
Disagree	2
Undecided	3
Agree	4
Strongly agree	5
NA	9

9. You shouldn't waste your time on anything that is not exciting.

	Col. 16
Strongly disagree	1
Disagree	2
Undecided	3
Agree	4
Strongly agree	5
NA	9

10. I like to succeed in the things that I do.

	Col. 17
Strongly disagree	1
Disagree	2
Undecided	3
Agree	4
Strongly agree	5
NA	9

11. I will never amount to anything worthwhile.

	Col. 18
Strongly disagree	1
Disagree	2
Undecided	3
Agree	4
Strongly agree	5
NA	9

12. Excitement makes life worth living.

	Col. 19
Strongly disagree	1
Disagree	2
Undecided	3
Agree	4
Strongly agree	5
NA	9

13. The easier the job, the better I like it.

	Col. 20
Strongly disagree	1
Disagree	2
Undecided	3
Agree	4
Strongly agree	5
NA	9

14. The more people know about me, the less they like me.

	Col. 21
Strongly disagree	1
Disagree	2
Undecided	3
Agree	4
Strongly agree	5
NA	9

15. You can get what you want from other people if you can outsmart them.

	Col. 22
Strongly disagree	1
Disagree	2
Undecided	3
Agree	4
Strongly agree	5
NA	9

16. I try to be better at things than most people.

	Col. 23
Strongly disagree	1
Disagree	2
Undecided	3
Agree	4
Strongly agree	5
NA	9

17. I don't believe that anyone really likes me.

	Col. 24
Strongly disagree	1
Disagree	2
Undecided	3
Agree	4
Strongly agree	5
NA	9

18. The most successful men got that way by being lucky.

	Col. 25
Strongly disagree	1
Disagree	2
Undecided	3
Agree	4
Strongly agree	5
NA	9

19. Doing hard jobs makes me proud.

	Col. 26
Strongly disagree	1
Disagree	2
Undecided	3
Agree	4
Strongly agree	5
NA	9

20. I'm not much good for anything.

	Col. 27
Strongly disagree	1
Disagree	2
Undecided	3
Agree	4
Strongly agree	5
NA	9

21. You've got to be able to fight your way out of tough spots.

	Col. 28
Strongly disagree	1
Disagree	2
Undecided	3
Agree	4
Strongly agree	5
NA	9

22. I don't like people who are always trying to get ahead.

	Col. 29
Strongly disagree	1
Disagree	2
Undecided	3
Agree	4
Strongly agree	5
NA	9

23. There's nothing about me that is any good.

	Col. 30
Strongly disagree	1
Disagree	2
Undecided	3
Agree	4
Strongly agree	5
NA	9

24. The only thing I have to look forward to is whatever excitement I can find.

	Col. 31
Strongly disagree	1
Disagree	2
Undecided	3
Agree	4
Strongly agree	5
NA	9

25. I would like to accomplish something of great significance.

	Col. 32
Strongly disagree	1
Disagree	2
Undecided	3
Agree	4
Strongly agree	5
NA	9

26. Sometimes, I think I'm no good at all.

	Col. 33
Strongly disagree	1
Disagree	2
Undecided	3
Agree	4
Strongly agree	5
NA	9

27. Anything that is not exciting is not worth doing.

	Col. 34
Strongly disagree	1
Disagree	2
Undecided	3
Agree	4
Strongly agree	5
NA	9

28. I like the challenge of a hard job.

	Col. 35
Strongly disagree	1
Disagree	2
Undecided	3
Agree	4
Strongly agree	5
NA	9

29. All in all, I would say that I am a failure.

	Col. 36
Strongly disagree	1
Disagree	2
Undecided	3
Agree	4
Strongly agree	5
NA	9

30. The tough guy has it made.

	Col. 37
Strongly disagree	1
Disagree	2
Undecided	3
Agree	4
Strongly agree	5
NA	9

31. The Parole Officer Aide (POA) can be a valuable assistant to the Parole Officer.

	Col. 38
Strongly disagree	1
Disagree	2
Undecided	3
Agree	4
Strongly agree	5
NA	9

32. The POA's prior criminal status will lessen his ability to line up jobs for parolees.

	Col. 39
Strongly disagree	1
Disagree	2
Undecided	3

	Col. 39
Agree	4
Strongly agree	5
NA	9

33. POAs have a unique understanding of problems of present parolees.

	Col. 40
Strongly disagree	1
Disagree	2
Undecided	3
Agree	4
Strongly agree	5
NA	9

34. There are few qualified POAs who can do effective parole work.

	Col. 41
Strongly disagree	1
Disagree	2
Undecided	3
Agree	4
Strongly agree	5
NA	9

35. POAs will be as effective in changing present parolees as are parole officers.

	Col. 42
Strongly disagree	1
Disagree	2
Undecided	3
Agree	4
Strongly agree	5
NA	9

36. POAs will undermine the parole officer's position with parolees.

	Col. 43
Strongly disagree	1
Disagree	2
Undecided	3
Agree	4
Strongly agree	5
NA	9

37. The best agent for changing parolees are POAs.

	Col. 44
Strongly disagree	1

Disagree	2
Undecided	3
Agree	4
Strongly agree	5
NA	9

38. Most parolees will see POAs as a stool pigeon for the correctional system.

	Col. 45
Strongly disagree	1
Disagree	2
Undecided	3
Agree	4
Strongly agree	5
NA	9

39. Use of POAs will improve the agency's public image.

	Col. 46
Strongly disagree	1
Disagree	2
Undecided	3
Agree	4
Strongly agree	5
NA	9

40. POAs will demand too much time and effort in supervision by parole officers.

	Col. 47
Strongly disagree	1
Disagree	2
Undecided	3
Agree	4
Strongly agree	5
NA	9

41. The use of POAs will probably result in new treatment programs that will help parolees adjust on the street.

	Col. 48
Strongly disagree	1
Disagree	2
Undecided	3
Agree	4
Strongly agree	5
NA	9

42. POAs will be torn between loyalties to the parolee and to the correctional agency.

	Col. 49
Strongly disagree	1
Disagree	2
Undecided	3
Agree	4
Strongly agree	5
NA	9

43. Using POAs is highly likely to reduce parole violations.

	Col. 50
Strongly disagree	1
Disagree	2
Undecided	3
Agree	4
Strongly agree	5
NA	9

44. POAs have little to offer the criminal justice system.

	Col. 51
Strongly disagree	1
Disagree	2
Undecided	3
Agree	4
Strongly agree	5
NA	9

45. In general, POAs are able to carry the same caseload as a parole officer.

	Col. 52
Strongly disagree	1
Disagree	2
Undecided	3
Agree	4
Strongly agree	5
NA	9

46. POAs would be more effective with multiple problem cases than with a general caseload.

	Col. 53
Strongly disagree	1
Disagree	2
Undecided	3

Agree	4
Strongly agree	5
NA	9

47. Most POAs will have problems relating to the average parole case.

	Col. 54
Strongly disagree	1
Disagree	2
Undecided	3
Agree	4
Strongly agree	5
NA	9

48. As far as the acceptance of other ex-offenders by the community is concerned, the use of POAs is likely to be useful to corrections.

	Col. 55
Strongly disagree	1
Disagree	2
Undecided	3
Agree	4
Strongly agree	5
NA	9

49. POAs would be more effective in institutional work rather than parole work.

	Col. 56
Strongly disagree	1
Disagree	2
Undecided	3
Agree	4
Strongly agree	5
NA	9

50. The POA will affect the image of the parole officer positively.

	Col. 57
Strongly disagree	1
Disagree	2
Undecided	3
Agree	4
Strongly agree	5
NA	9

51. Most parolees would object to being supervised by a POA rather than a parole officer.

	Col. 58
Strongly disagree	1
Disagree	2
Undecided	3
Agree	4
Strongly agree	5
NA	9

52. POAs decrease the gap between parolees and the parole system.

	Col. 59
Strongly disagree	1
Disagree	2
Undecided	3
Agree	4
Strongly agree	5
NA	9

53. The POA will affect the image of the parole officer negatively.

	Col. 60
Strongly disagree	1
Disagree	2
Undecided	3
Agree	4
Strongly agree	5
NA	9

54. POAs are able to promote positive public relations for the parole system.

	Col. 61
Strongly disagree	1
Disagree	2
Undecided	3
Agree	4
Strongly agree	5
NA	9

55. Using POAs will not increase trust of parolees in the parole system.

	Col. 62
Strongly disagree	1
Disagree	2
Undecided	3
Agree	4
Strongly agree	5
NA	9

56. Parolees who are assisted by POAs are more likely to succeed on parole than those who do not receive such help.

	Col. 63
Strongly disagree	1
Disagree	2
Undecided	3
Agree	4
Strongly agree	5
NA	9

57. POAs will not be as effective as the parole officer since the parolee will not see him as an authority figure.

	Col. 64
Strongly disagree	1
Disagree	2
Undecided	3
Agree	4
Strongly agree	5
NA	9

58. POAs can establish productive relations with non-middle class parolees.

	Col. 65
Strongly disagree	1
Disagree	2
Undecided	3
Agree	4
Strongly agree	5
NA	9

59. Most POAs tend to overlook technical violations of parolees.

	Col. 66
Strongly disagree	1
Disagree	2
Undecided	3
Agree	4
Strongly agree	5
NA	9

60. It is easy for a POA to help parolees avoid pitfalls which he has already made.

	Col. 67
Strongly disagree	1
Disagree	2

	Col. 67
Undecided	3
Agree	4
Strongly agree	5
NA	9

61. Most POAs will not be as dedicated to changing parolees as will parole officers.

	Col. 68
Strongly disagree	1
Disagree	2
Undecided	3
Agree	4
Strongly agree	5
NA	9

62. Using POAs will increase trust of parolees in the parole system.

	Col. 69
Strongly disagree	1
Disagree	2
Undecided	3
Agree	4
Strongly agree	5
NA	9

63. POAs are as effective in changing behavior of parolees as are parole officers.

	Col. 70
Strongly disagree	1
Disagree	2
Undecided	3
Agree	4
Strongly agree	5
NA	9

64. Parole officers are more effective in changing behavior of parolees than are POAs.

	Col. 71
Strongly disagree	1
Disagree	2
Undecided	3
Agree	4
Strongly agree	5
NA	9

117

65. The use of POAs can reduce recidivism among parolees.

	Col. 72
Strongly disagree	1
Disagree	2
Undecided	3
Agree	4
Strongly agree	5
NA	9

66. POAs can supervise parolees with a minimum of difficulty.

	Col. 73
Strongly disagree	1
Disagree	2
Undecided	3
Agree	4
Strongly agree	5
NA	9

CARD 2

Study number: Col. 1

2

Card number: Col. 2

2

Case number: Cols. 3-5

67. In general, the use of ex-offenders in corrections should be discouraged.

	Col. 6
Strongly disagree	1
Disagree	2
Undecided	3
Agree	4
Strongly agree	5
NA	9

68. Increased parole supervision will reduce recidivism among parolees.

	Col. 7
Strongly disagree	1
Disagree	2

	Col. 7
Undecided	3
Agree	4
Strongly agree	5
NA	9

69. For the most part, I favor the methadone maintenance principle for heroin addicts.

	Col. 8
Strongly disagree	1
Disagree	2
Undecided	3
Agree	4
Strongly agree	5
NA	9

70. I favor the use of ex-offenders in corrections.

	Col. 9
Strongly disagree	1
Disagree	2
Undecided	3
Agree	4
Strongly agree	5
NA	9

71. Bringing about a matching of supervisional style with offender type is more important in parole work than is simply reducing caseloads.

	Col. 10
Strongly disagree	1
Disagree	2
Undecided	3
Agree	4
Strongly agree	5
NA	9

72. Abortion should be legalized.

	Col. 11
Strongly disagree	1
Disagree	2
Undecided	3
Agree	4
Strongly agree	5
NA	9

73. In general, the use of ex-offenders in corrections should be encouraged.

	Col. 12
Strongly disagree	1
Disagree	2
Undecided	3
Agree	4
Strongly agree	5
NA	9

74. Reducing caseloads is more important in parole work than is bringing about a match of supervisional style with offender type.

	Col. 13
Strongly disagree	1
Disagree	2
Undecided	3
Agree	4
Strongly agree	5
NA	9

75. In general, using the product of a social problem to deal with that social problem can be effective in corrections.

	Col. 14
Strongly disagree	1
Disagree	2
Undecided	3
Agree	4
Strongly agree	5
NA	9

76. Sexual relations between consenting adults in private should be legalized.

	Col. 15
Strongly disagree	1
Disagree	2
Undecided	3
Agree	4
Strongly agree	5
NA	9

77. Non-support of families should be handled as a non-criminal problem, rather than as a crime.

	Col. 16
Strongly disagree	1
Disagree	2

	Col. 16
Undecided	3
Agree	4
Strongly agree	5
NA	9

78. Private use of marijuana in the home should not be a felony offense.

	Col. 17
Strongly disagree	1
Disagree	2
Undecided	3
Agree	4
Strongly agree	5
NA	9

79. Marijuana should be legalized.

	Col. 18
Strongly disagree	1
Disagree	2
Undecided	3
Agree	4
Strongly agree	5
NA	9

80. Most public officials (people in public office) are not really interested in the problems of the average man. In general, would you agree with that statement or disagree?

	Col. 19
Agree	0
Disagree	1
NA	9

81. These days a person doesn't really know whom he can count on.

	Col. 20
Agree	0
Disagree	1
NA	9

82. Nowadays a person has to live pretty much for today and let tomorrow take care of itself.

	Col. 21
Agree	0
Disagree	1
NA	9

83. In spite of what some people say, the lot (condition) of the average man is getting worse, not better.

	Col. 22
Agree	0
Disagree	1
NA	9

84. It's hardly fair to bring a child into the world with the way things look for the future.

	Col. 23
Agree	0
Disagree	1
NA	9

85. There's very little we can do to keep prices from going higher.

	Col. 24
Agree	0
Disagree	1
NA	9

86. Persons like myself have little chance of protecting their personal interests when they conflict with those of strong pressure groups.

	Col. 25
Agree	0
Disagree	1
NA	9

87. A lasting world peace can be achieved by those of us who work toward it.

	Col. 26
Agree	0
Disagree	1
NA	9

88. I think each of us can do a great deal to improve world opinion of the United States.

	Col. 27
Agree	0
Disagree	1
NA	9

89. This world is run by the few people in power, and there is not much the little guy can do about it.

	Col. 28
Agree	0
Disagree	1
NA	9

90. People like me can change the course of world events if we make ourselves heard.

	Col. 29
Agree	0
Disagree	1
NA	9

91. More and more, I feel helpless in the face of what's happening in the world today.

	Col. 30
Agree	0
Disagree	1
NA	9

92. If you start trying to change things very much, you usually make them worse.

	Col. 31
Agree	0
Disagree	1
NA	9

93. No matter how we like to talk about it, political authority really comes not from us, but from some higher power.

	Col. 32
Agree	0
Disagree	1
NA	9

94. It's better to stick by what you have than to be trying new things you don't really know about.

	Col. 33
Agree	0
Disagree	1
NA	9

95. A man doesn't really get to have much wisdom until he's well along in years.

	Col. 34
Agree	0
Disagree	1
NA	9

96. I prefer the *practical* man anytime to the man of ideas.

	Col. 35
Agree	0
Disagree	1
NA	9

97. Fundamentally, the world we live in is a pretty lonely place.

	Col. 36
Agree very much	0
Agree on the whole	1
Agree a little	2
Disagree a little	3
Disagree on the whole	4
Disagree very much	5
NA	9

98. It is often desirable to reserve judgment about what's going on.

	Col. 37
Agree very much	0
Agree on the whole	1
Agree a little	2
Disagree a little	3
Disagree on the whole	4
Disagree very much	5
NA	9

99. A person who thinks primarily of his own happiness is beneath contempt.

	Col. 38
Agree very much	0
Agree on the whole	1
Agree a little	2
Disagree a little	3
Disagree on the whole	4
Disagree very much	5
NA	9

100. In the history of mankind there have probably been just a handful of really great thinkers.

	Col. 39
Agree very much	0
Agree on the whole	1

	Col. 39
Agree a little	2
Disagree a little	3
Disagree on the whole	4
Disagree very much	5
NA	9

101. Most people don't know what's good for them.

	Col. 40
Agree very much	0
Agree on the whole	1
Agree a little	2
Disagree a little	3
Disagree on the whole	4
Disagree very much	5
NA	9

102. Once I get wound up in a heated discussion I just can't stop.

	Col. 41
Agree very much	0
Agree on the whole	1
Agree a little	2
Disagree a little	3
Disagree on the whole	4
Disagree very much	5
NA	9

103. The worst crime a person can commit is to attack publicly the people who believe in the same thing he does.

	Col. 42
Agree very much	0
Agree on the whole	1
Agree a little	2
Disagree a little	3
Disagree on the whole	4
Disagree very much	5
NA	9

104. In this complicated world of ours the only way we know what is going on is to rely upon leaders or experts who can be trusted.

	Col. 43
Agree very much	0
Agree on the whole	1

Agree a little	2
Disagree a little	3
Disagree on the whole	4
Disagree very much	5
NA	9

105. In the long run the best way to live is to pick friends and associates whose tastes and beliefs are the same as one's own.

	Col. 44
Agree very much	0
Agree on the whole	1
Agree a little	2
Disagree a little	3
Disagree on the whole	4
Disagree very much	5
NA	9

106. While I don't like to admit this even to myself, I sometimes have the ambition to become a great man like Einstein, Beethoven, or Shakespeare.

	Col. 45
Agree very much	0
Agree on the whole	1
Agree a little	2
Disagree a little	3
Disagree on the whole	4
Disagree very much	5
NA	9

107. My blood boils whenever a person stubbornly refuses to admit he's wrong.

	Col. 46
Agree very much	0
Agree on the whole	1
Agree a little	2
Disagree a little	3
Disagree on the whole	4
Disagree very much	5
NA	9

108. There are two kinds of people in this world: those who are for the truth and those who are against the truth.

	Col. 47
Agree very much	0
Agree on the whole	1

	Col. 47
Agree a little	2
Disagree a little	3
Disagree on the whole	4
Disagree very much	5
NA	9

109. Man on his own is a helpless and miserable creature.

	Col. 48
Agree very much	0
Agree on the whole	1
Agree a little	2
Disagree a little	3
Disagree on the whole	4
Disagree very much	5
NA	9

110. It is better to be a dead hero than to be a live coward.

	Col. 49
Agree very much	0
Agree on the whole	1
Agree a little	2
Disagree a little	3
Disagree on the whole	4
Disagree very much	5
NA	9

111. The present is all too often full of unhappiness. It is only the future that counts.

	Col. 50
Agree very much	0
Agree on the whole	1
Agree a little	2
Disagree a little	3
Disagree on the whole	4
Disagree very much	5
NA	9

112. If something grows up over a long time, there will always be much wisdom in it.

	Col. 51
Agree very much	0
Agree on the whole	1
Agree a little	2

Disagree a little	3
Disagree on the whole	4
Disagree very much	5
NA	9

113. I'd want to know that something would really work before I'd be willing to take a chance on it.

	Col. 52
Agree very much	0
Agree on the whole	1
Agree a little	2
Disagree a little	3
Disagree on the whole	4
Disagree very much	5
NA	9

114. All groups can live in harmony in this country without changing the system in any way.

	Col. 53
Agree very much	0
Agree on the whole	1
Agree a little	2
Disagree a little	3
Disagree on the whole	4
Disagree very much	5
NA	9

115. We must respect the work of our forefathers and not think that we know better than they did.

	Col. 54
Agree very much	0
Agree on the whole	1
Agree a little	2
Disagree a little	3
Disagree on the whole	4
Disagree very much	5
NA	9

116. On the whole, people in Ohio are in favor of a more lenient approach in handling convicted adult felon offenders than is presently practiced.

	Col. 55
Agree very much	0
Agree on the whole	1

	Col. 55
Agree a little	2
Disagree a little	3
Disagree on the whole	4
Disagree very much	5
NA	9

117. What proportion of offenders sent to prison do you believe to be mentally ill, although not necessarily legally insane?

	Col. 56
Most offenders	1
A significant minority	2
None or very few	3
Don't know	4
NA	9

118. First, how important is *reformation* in your evaluation of corrections today? Reformation refers to the attempt to change the offender through treatment of corrective measures, so that when given the chance he will refrain from committing crime.

	Col. 57
Very important	1
Quite important	2
Some importance	3
Little importance	4
No importance	5
NA	9

119. In your evaluation as to the purpose of corrections today, how important should *general deterrence* be? By general deterrence we mean the attempt to impose a penalty on the offender sufficiently severe that potential offenders among the general public will refrain from committing crime through the fear of punishment.

	Col. 58
Very important	1
Quite important	2
Some importance	3
Little importance	4
No importance	5
NA	9

120. How important should *individual deterrence* be? By individual deterrence we mean the attempt to impose a penalty on the offender sufficiently *severe* that he will refrain from committing further crime through the fear of punishment.

	Col. 59
Very important	1
Quite important	2
Some importance	3
Little importance	4
No importance	5
NA	9

121. How important should *punishment* be? By punishment we mean the attempt to make the punishment more an object of dread than the offense is an object of desire, irrespective of whether the penalty will deter subsequent crimes.

	Col. 60
Very important	1
Quite important	2
Some importance	3
Little importance	4
No importance	5
NA	9

122. How important should *incapacitation* be? By incapacitation we mean the attempt to protect society for a period of time by removing the offender from the community and placing him in prison.

	Col. 61
Very important	1
Quite important	2
Some importance	3
Little importance	4
No importance	5
NA	9

123. In the course of your experience you have had occasion to observe many offenders. What conclusions have you come to concerning the causes of crime? (Be as specific as possible.)

	Col. 62
Situational factors	
Society, kicks, excitement	0
Biological factors	
Heredity, minority groups, mental deficiency	1
Social factors	
Lower-class, poor, poorly educated, irresponsible parents, bad marriage	2

	Col. 62
Chemical substances	
Drugs, alcohol	3
NA	9

124. If it were your task to differentiate between good parole officers and inadequate ones, what criteria would you use in identifying the good ones?

	Col. 63
Strong and firm individual	0
Altruistic individual who can	
empathize	1
Low return rate	2
NA	9

125. What is your age? _____

	Cols. 64-65
NA	99

126. What is your marital status?

	Col. 66
Married	0
Divorced or separated	1
Single	2
NA	9

127. What was your father's usual job or occupation while you were growing up?

	Col. 67
Unskilled employees	1
Machine operators & semi-skilled	
employees	2
Skilled manual employees	3
Clerical and sales workers	4
Administrative personnel, owners	
of small businesses, minor	
professionals	5
Business managers	6
Higher executives	7
NA	9

128. If in parole work, how long have you been in the service?

	Col. 68
Under 6 months	1

More than 6 months, but less than one year	2
1-2 years	3
3 years or more	4
NA	9

129. How much formal education have you completed?

Col. 69

Less than high school	1
High school graduate	2
2 years or less of college	3
More than 2 years of college	4
College degree	5
Graduate studies	6
NA	9

130. Have you attended any parole workshops or training programs other than in-service orientation programs?

Col. 70

Yes	0
No	1
NA	9

131. Do you plan to make a career of correctional work?

Col. 71

Yes	0
No	1
NA	9

132. Race

Col. 72

White	0
Black	1
NA	9

133. Sex

Col. 73

Male	0
Female	1
NA	9

134. Position with APA?

Col. 74

Parole Officer Aide	0
Parole Officer	1
NA	9

Interview Form for Parole Officer Aides

Interviewer _____

Date _____ Time Begin _____ Time End _____

Total Time _____

Study Number:	Col. 1
	3
Card Number:	Col. 2
	1
Case Number:	Cols. 2-5

Region office:	Cols. 6-7
Canton	00
Columbus	01
Akron	02
Youngstown	03
Cleveland	04
Cincinnati	05
Lima	06
Athens	07
Dayton	08
Toledo	09

1. In general, what portion of your work is directly supervised by someone else on a regular basis? Would you say none of it, very little, about one-fourth, about half, about three fourths, or almost all of it?

   If Necessary: For what portion of your work are you directly accountable to someone else?

	Col. 8
No supervision	0
Very little	1
One-fourth	2
Half	3

133

	Col. 8
Three-fourths	4
Almost all	5
Directly supervised, but can't say how much	7
INAP (R not in the labor force)	8
DK; NA	9

2. How clearly defined are your responsibilities and duties as a parole aid?

	Col. 9
They are as clearly defined as they should be	0
Almost as clearly as they should be	1
They should be defined somewhat more clearly	2
They should be defined more clearly	3
They should be defined much more clearly	4
Other	7
DK; NA	9

3. On the whole, how satisfied are you with your present job, when you consider the expectations you had when you started it? Would you say that you are now very dissatisfied, slightly dissatisfied, moderately satisfied, or very satisfied with your job?

	Col. 10
Very dissatisfied	0
Slightly dissatisfied	1
Neutral	2
Moderately satisfied	3
Very satisfied	4
Don't know	7
INAP (R not in the labor force)	8
NA	9

4. On a typical day, how many people at work do you actually talk with about personal interests, family activities, sports events, and similar topics?

	Col. 11
None	0
1 - 2 persons	1
3 - 4 persons	2
5 - 6 persons	3
7 - 9 persons	4
10 - 14 persons	5
15 or more persons	6
Talk with people, but can't say how many	7
INAP (R not in the labor force, or not friends at work)	8
DK; NA	9

5. At work, how many co-workers do you know well enough to take a coffee
    break with or eat lunch with, on a fairly regular basis?

    Col. 12

None (regardless of R's opportunities to do this)	0
1 - 2 persons	1
3 - 4 persons	2
5 - 6 persons	3
7 - 9 persons	4
10 - 14 persons	5
15 or more persons	6
Know some people, but can't say how many	7
INAP (R not in the labor force)	8
DK; NA	9

Now we have a number of questions about your job. There are no right or wrong
answers, we would simply like to know how you feel about certain things. After
I read each statement please look at Card 1 (Give R Card 1) and tell me which
response you choose. That is, do you (A) strongly disagree (B) mildly disagree
(C) mildly agree or (D) strongly agree. Here is the first statement.

6. There are good opportunities here for those who want to get ahead.

    Col. 13

A.	Strongly disagree	0
B.	Mildly disagree	1
	Neutral; both agree and disagree	2
C.	Mildly agree	3
D.	Strongly agree	4
E.	Don't know; no opinion	7
	NA	9

7. The longer you work here the more you feel you belong.

    Col. 14

A.	Strongly disagree	0
B.	Mildly disagree	1
	Neutral; both agree and disagree	2
C.	Mildly agree	3
D.	Strongly agree	4
E.	Don't know; no opinion	7
	NA	9

8. Many of the rules here are annoying.

    Col. 15

A.	Strongly disagree	0
B.	Mildly disagree	1

		Col. 15
	Neutral; both agree and disagree	2
C.	Mildly agree	3
D.	Strongly agree	4
E.	Don't know; no opinion	7
	NA	9

9. I plan to continue working here until I retire.

		Col. 16
A.	Strongly disagree	0
B.	Mildly disagree	1
	Neutral; both agree and disagree	2
C.	Mildly agree	3
D.	Strongly agree	4
E.	Don't know; no opinion	7
	NA	9

10. I feel that my job is no more interesting than others I could get.

		Col. 17
A.	Strongly disagree	0
B.	Mildly disagree	1
	Neutral; both agree and disagree	2
C.	Mildly agree	3
D.	Strongly agree	4
E.	Don't know; no opinion	7
	NA	9

11. How things are done here is usually left up to the person doing the work.

		Col. 18
A.	Strongly disagree	0
B.	Mildly disagree	1
	Neutral; both agree and disagree	2
C.	Mildly agree	3
D.	Strongly agree	4
E.	Don't know; no opinion	7
	NA	9

12. In the usual case, only general guidelines are given and a person works out the details of the job for himself.

		Col. 19
A.	Strongly disagree	0
B.	Mildly disagree	1
	Neutral; both agree and disagree	2
C.	Mildly agree	3

D.	Strongly agree	4
E.	Don't know; no opinion	7
	NA	9

13. My position gives me a chance to try out new ideas.

Col. 20

A.	Strongly disagree	0
B.	Mildly disagree	1
	Neutral; both agree and disagree	2
C.	Mildly agree	3
D.	Strongly agree	4
E.	Don't know; no opinion	7
	NA	9

14. I feel that I am my own boss in most matters concerning the job.

Col. 21

A.	Strongly disagree	0
B.	Mildly disagree	1
	Neutral; both agree and disagree	2
C.	Mildly agree	3
D.	Strongly agree	4
E.	Don't know; no opinion	7
	NA	9

15. Any decision I make concerning parolees has to have my supervisor's approval.

Col. 22

A.	Strongly disagree	0
B.	Mildly disagree	1
	Neutral; both agree and disagree	2
C.	Mildly agree	3
D.	Strongly agree	4
E.	Don't know; no opinion	7
	NA	9

16. I have to account for my actions on the job to my supervisor.

Col. 23

A.	Strongly disagree	0
B.	Mildly disagree	1
	Neutral; both agree and disagree	2
C.	Mildly agree	3
D.	Strongly agree	4
E.	Don't know; no opinion	7
	NA	9

17. Even small decisions concerning parolees have to be referred to someone higher up for a final answer.

		Col. 24
A.	Strongly disagree	0
B.	Mildly disagree	1
	Neutral; both agree and disagree	2
C.	Strongly agree	3
D.	Don't know; no opinion	7
	NA	9

18. There can be little action taken here until a decision is approved by a supervisor.

		Col. 25
A.	Strongly disagree	0
B.	Mildly disagree	1
	Neutral; both agree and disagree	2
C.	Mildly agree	3
D.	Strongly agree	4
E.	Don't know; no opinion	7
	NA	9

19. I feel that I do not have enough autonomy (freedom) to do my job well.

		Col. 26
A.	Strongly disagree	0
B.	Mildly disagree	1
	Neutral; both agree and disagree	2
C.	Mildly agree	3
D.	Strongly agree	4
E.	Don't know; no opinion	7
	NA	9

20. A person who wants to make his own decisions would be quickly discouraged here.

		Col. 27
A.	Strongly disagree	0
B.	Mildly disagree	1
	Neutral; both agree and disagree	2
C.	Mildly agree	3
D.	Strongly agree	4
E.	Don't know; no opinion	7
	NA	9

139

21. Most of the supervisors here leave you alone as long as you do your job.

Col. 28

A.	Strongly disagree	0
B.	Mildly disagree	1
	Neutral; both agree and disagree	2
C.	Mildly agree	3
D.	Strongly agree	4
E.	Don't know; no opinion	7
	NA	9

Take Card (# 1) From Respondent

22. How satisfied are you with your fellow workers?

Col. 29

Very dissatisfied	0
Slightly dissatisfied	1
Neutral	2
Moderately satisfied	3
Very satisfied	4
Don't know	7
NA	9

23. How satisfied are you with your present supervisor?

Col. 30

Very dissatisfied	0
Slightly dissatisfied	1
Neutral	2
Moderately satisfied	3
Very satisfied	4
Don't know	7
NA	9

24. How satisfied are you with the amount of freedom (autonomy) you have in your job?

Col. 31

Very dissatisfied	0
Slightly dissatisfied	1
Neutral	2
Moderately satisfied	3
Very satisfied	4
Don't know	7
NA	9

25. On the whole, to what extent do the people in your office make you feel that you are an important member of the "parole team"?

	Col.32
Not at all	0
To a small extent	1
To a fair extent	2
To a great extent	4
NA, DK	9

26. How easy is it for you to get together and exchange information and ideas about work problems with the following staff members? Would you say (read choices to R):

	Very easy (1)	Fairly easy (2)	Not as easy as it could be (3)	Rather difficult (4)	Very difficult (5)	
Unit supervisor						Col. 33
Senior parole officer						Col. 34
Other parole officers						Col. 35

27. Do you feel as if you could do a better job if you were given more authority than you now have?

Col. 36

Why? (Write Respondent's answer out)

Col. 37

28. In your opinion, what are some of the most important problems in the Adult Parole Authority?

Col. 38

29. About how often do you confer with your fellow workers regarding the proper handling of a parolee or other problems?

Col. 39

What reasons do you generally have for conferring with your fellow workers?

Col. 40

30. Why do you continue to work for the Adult Parole Authority?

Col. 41

31. About how often do you confer with your supervisor(s) regarding the proper handling of a parolee?

Col. 42

What kinds of decisions do you *usually* refer to your supervisor?

Col. 43

Are you required to do this or do you do it voluntarily?

Col. 44

32. Roughly, what percent of your time do you spend in the following activities during the average week?

Col. 45

Direct face-to-face parole contact or supervision

Col. 46

Committee meetings

Col. 47

Administration (scheduling, planning, paperwork)

Col. 48

Self-training, studying, etc.

Col. 49

Other (what)

33. What do you like least about your job?   Col. 50

34. What do you like most about your job?   Col. 51

35. What is your present marital status?   Col. 52

Married	0
Single	1
Divorced	2
Separated	3
Widowed	4
NA	9

36. Do you have a religious preference?

If yes: What is your preference?   Col. 53

142

	Col. 53
No preference (or atheist or agnostic or undecided)	0
Protestant (regardless of denomination)	1
Catholic	2
Jewish	3
Orthodox	4
Other religion (specify)_____	5
NA	9

If Respondent is Protestant (Ask only if necessary):

What denomination do you prefer?

_____

(Record exact name of denomination given by R.)

37. Are you now a member of a local church or synagogue?

	Col. 54
No	0
Yes	1
DK; NA	9

38. About how often do you usually attend religious services?

	Col. 55
Never	0
Few times a year	1
Once a month	2
2 or 3 times a month	3
Once a week	4
More than once a week	5
Attend; but can't say how often	7
DK; NA	9

39. Some people wonder whether there is a God. How do you feel—do you think that there is not a God, do you have some doubts that there is a God, are you certain that there is a God, or do you think it is impossible for man to know anything about this?

	Col. 56
Do not believe	0
Agnostic	1
Have doubts	2
Certain	3
Humanistic or scientific conceptions of a supreme being or cosmic order	4

	Col. 56
Don't know, don't care	7
NA	9

If Respondent believes in God, regardless of doubts:

Do you believe that after this life God will reward some people and punish others?

	Col. 57
No	0
Maybe, or not sure	1
Yes	2
NA	9

40. What was your father's usual job or occupation while you were growing up?

Col. 58

If Necessary: What kind of work did he do?

_____

(Be as specific as possible—determine the exact job title. DK = 7; NA = 9.)

41. How many years of school did you complete, including any vocational training?

	Col. 59
0 - 3 years	0
4 - 6 years	1
7 - 8 years	2
9 - 11 years (some high school or trade school)	3
12 years (high school graduate)	4
13 - 15 years (some college or technical school)	5
16 years (college graduate)	6
17 - 18 years (M.A. or some graduate work)	7
19 or more years (M.D., Ph.D., L.L.B., etc.)	8
DK; NA	9

42. How many years of schooling did your father complete?

	Col. 60
0 - 3 years	0
4 - 6 years	1
7 - 8 years	2
9 - 11 years (some high school or trade school)	3
12 years (high school graduate)	4

	Col. 60
13 - 15 years (some college or technical school)	5
16 years (college graduate)	6
17 - 18 years (MA or some graduate work)	7
19 or more years (M.D., Ph.D., L.L.B., etc.)	8
DK; NA	9

43. How many years of schooling did your mother complete?

	Col. 61
0 - 3 years	0
4 - 6 years	1
7 - 8 years	2
9 - 11 years (some high school or trade school)	3
12 years (high school graduate)	4
13 - 15 years (some college or technical school)	5
16 years (college graduate)	6
17 - 18 years (MA or some graduate work)	7
19 or more years (M.D., Ph.D., L.L.B., etc.)	8
DK; NA	9

44. On your last birthday, how old were you? _____ Cols. 62-63

45. Finally, the last few questions deal with the law and legal practices. First, do you feel that the laws dealing with criminal offenses in Ohio are too lenient, too severe, or about right?

	Col. 64
Too lenient	0
About right	1
Too severe	2
Don't know, no opinion	7
NA	9

46. What is your thinking about the use of the death penalty in Ohio? Should the death penalty be used more often than it is now, less often than now, or should it be completely abolished?

	Col. 65
More often	0
As often as now	1
Less often	2
Abolished	3
Don't know, no opinion	7
NA	9

47. How serious do you feel the crime problem in Ohio is?

	Col. 66
Not very serious	0
Quite serious	1
Most serious problem in the state	2
DK; NA	9

48. Which program would help most to reduce the crime problem in Ohio?

	Col. 67
Better education or employment opportunities, social and psychiatric help, more study of crime causes	0
Emphasis on moral standards, pass more laws, stiffer penalties, put religion back into schools	1
DK; NA	9

49. Under which circumstance do you believe crime is least likely? When the suspect is likely to be caught and given a mild penalty or when there will be a severe penalty for those caught but one is unlikely to be apprehended?

	Col. 68
Likely to be caught, mild penalty	0
Severe penalty, unlikely to be caught	1
DK; NA	9

50. What is your opinion on the proportion of offenders sent to prison?

	Col. 69
Not enough get prison terms	0
About right number get prison sentences	1
Too many are sent to prison	2
DK; NA	9

51. How much time should prisoners serve, on the average?

	Col. 70
1 1/2 years or less	0
3 years	1
5 years	2
10 years	3
DK; NA	9

52. Do you approve of "plea copping"? (Reducing the formal charges against a suspect in return for his agreement to plead guilty.)

	Col. 71
Strongly approve	0

	Col. 71
Approve	1
Disapprove	2
Strongly disapprove	3
DK; NA	9

53. Do you have any close friends who have been the victim of a major crime?

	Col. 72
Yes	0
No	1
DK; NA	9

	Col. 1
Study Number:	3

	Col. 2
Card Number:	2

	Cols. 3-5
Case Number:	

54. People have very different feelings about the police and the law. I'll read a number of statements that are sometimes made about legal and police practices. After each statement, please look again at Card 1 (Refer R to Card 1) and tell me whether you strongly disagree, mildly disagree, mildly agree, or strongly agree with the statement.

Almost anything can be fixed in courts if you have money.

	Col. 6
Strongly disagree	0
Mildly disagree	1
Neutral; both agree and disagree	2
Mildly agree	3
Strongly agree	4
Don't know; no opinion	7
NA	9

55. Cops often carry a grudge against men who get in trouble with the law and treat them cruelly.

	Col. 7
Strongly disagree	0

Mildly disagree	1
Neutral; both agree and disagree	2
Mildly agree	3
Strongly agree	4
Don't know; no opinion	7
NA	9

56. A policeman usually judges you as guilty.

Col. 8

Strongly disagree	0
Mildly disagree	1
Neutral; both agree and disagree	2
Mildly agree	3
Strongly agree	7
NA	9

57. Prosecutors are nothing but politicians.

Col. 9

Strongly disagree	0
Mildly disagree	1
Neutral; both agree and disagree	2
Mildly agree	3
Strongly agree	4
Don't know; no opinion	7
NA	9

58. Police should periodically search houses of known criminals.

Col. 10

Strongly agree	0
Agree	1
Disagree	2
Strongly disagree	3
DK; NA	9

59. Police should not question suspects without advising them of the right to be silent.

Col. 11

Strongly agree	0
Agree	1
Disagree	2
Strongly disagree	3
DK; NA	9

60. When the police catch a person for a crime they should search him, his car, etc., for evidence of other crimes.

	Col. 12
Strongly agree	0
Agree	1
Disagree	2
Strongly disagree	3
DK; NA	9

61. The police should use any necessary technique to catch criminals who commit robberies, etc.

	Col. 13
Strongly agree	0
Agree	1
Disagree	2
Strongly disagree	3
DK; NA	9

62. Police should be allowed to "rough up" rape suspects to get confessions from them.

	Col. 14
Strongly agree	0
Agree	1
Disagree	2
Strongly disagree	3
DK; NA	9

63. Police should not arrest skid row drunks solely for drunkenness.

	Col. 15
Strongly agree	0
Agree	1
Disagree	2
Strongly disagree	3
DK; NA	9

64. Police and courts are almost always fair with accused persons.

	Col. 16
Strongly agree	0
Agree	1
Disagree	2
Strongly disagree	3
DK; NA	9

65. Police know who the people are that make their living committing burglaries, robberies, etc.

	Col. 17
Strongly agree	0
Agree	1
Disagree	2
Strongly disagree	3
DK; NA	9

66. The state should provide attorneys to persons arrested for all serious crimes.

	Col. 18
Strongly agree	0
Agree	1
Disagree	2
Strongly disagree	3
DK; NA	9

67. The state should provide attorneys to persons arrested for all minor crimes.

	Col. 19
Strongly agree	0
Agree	1
Disagree	2
Strongly disagree	3
DK; NA	9

68. Supreme Court decisions hindered the police in efforts to fight crime.

	Col. 20
Strongly agree	0
Agree	1
Disagree	2
Strongly disagree	3
DK; NA	9

69. Criminals should not be executed.

	Col. 21
Strongly agree	0
Agree	1
Disagree	2
Strongly disagree	3
DK; NA	9

70. Do you approve of releasing accused suspects on their "own recognizance"?

	Col. 22
Strongly approve	0
Approve	1
Disapprove	2
Strongly disapprove	3
DK; NA	9

71. What is your opinion of having halfway houses in your neighborhood?

	Col. 23
Strongly support	0
Support	1
Oppose	2
Strongly oppose	3
DK; NA	9

72. How much time do prisoners serve in state prisons, on the average?

	Col. 24
1 1/2 years or less	0
3 years	1
5 years	2
10 years	3
DK; NA	9

73. How well are state juvenile correctional workers doing their job?

	Col. 25
Very well	0
Reasonably well	1
Somewhat poorly	2
Very poorly	3
DK; NA	9

74. How well are state adult correctional workers doing their job?

	Col. 26
Very well	0
Reasonably well	1
Somewhat poorly	2
Very poorly	3
DK; NA	9

The following questions deal with parole. I would like you to simply indicate whether you agree or disagree with each statement. The first statement is:

75. The average prisoner released from prison on parole has got a good break. He should make it on his own without help from here on. Do you agree or disagree?

	Col. 27
Agree	0
Disagree	1
Not sure	2
DK; NA	9

76. The average prisoner released from prison on parole needs some help in making a go of his parole.

	Col. 28
Agree	0
Disagree	1
Not sure	2
DK; NA	9

77. A guy on parole should be left alone to work out things for himself and not be bugged by a parole officer.

	Col. 29
Agree	0
Disagree	1
Not sure	2
DK; NA	9

78. If the average parole officer had a smaller load of cases and had more time to help his parolees with their problems, this would be a good thing.

	Col. 30
Agree	0
Disagree	1
Not sure	2
DK; NA	9

79. If Ohio was able to get some volunteers to help parole officers with their parolees, this would be a good thing.

	Col. 31
Agree	0
Disagree	1
Not sure	2
DK; NA	9

80. Would the average citizen think volunteer parole work would take too much of his time?

	Col. 32
Yes	0
No	1
Not sure	2
DK; NA	9

81. Would the average citizen think volunteer work with ex-prisoners (parolees) would be dangerous?

	Col. 33
Yes	0
No	1
Not sure	2
DK; NA	9

82. As a part of this study, we are also trying to find out how well political figures and issues are publicized. For instance, who is John J. Gilligan?

Col. 34

Correct Answer: John J. Gilligan, Governor of Ohio.

Incorrect; don't know	0
Correct	1
NA	9

83. What are the names of the two U.S. Senators from Ohio?

Col. 35

Correct Answers: Robert Taft and William Saxbe

Neither name correct; don't know	0
One name correct (only last name necessary)	1
Both names correct (only last names necessary)	2
NA	9

84. Have you ever done any sort of volunteer work for a political party or a candidate?

Col. 36

If yes: Have you done volunteer work in one election, two elections, or more than that?

Never	0
One election	1
Two elections	2
Three or more elections	3
Worked, but don't remember how many times	7
DK; NA	9

85. Did you vote in the last election for President of the U.S.?

> If yes: Did you vote for Richard Nixon (for the Republican candidate) or for George McGovern (for the Democratic candidate) or for someone else?

> If no: Were you registered to vote in that election?

> If not registered: Were you eligible to register at that time?

	Col. 37
Voted for Richard Nixon (the Rep. candidate)	0
Voted for George McGovern (the Dem. candidate)	1
Voted for someone else	2
Voted, but don't remember or won't say for whom	3
Did not vote, but registered	4
Not registered, but eligible	5
Not eligible	6
Not registered, but don't know if eligible	7
DK; NA	9

86. In national elections, do you consider yourself a Republican, a Democrat, an Independent, or do you have some other political preference?

	Col. 38
Republican	0
Democrat	1
Independent	2
Other (specify)	3
No preference	4
NA	9

87. If a group of people in this country strongly feels that they are being treated unfairly, what kinds of actions do you think they have the right to take in trying to change the situation? I will read a list of different kinds of actions that dissatisfied groups sometimes take. After each action, please tell me whether or not you think dissatisfied groups have the right to do this, regardless of how you personally feel about it.

Hold public meetings and rallies	Col. 39
No	0
Yes	1
Don't know, it depends	2
NA	9

88. March quietly and peacefully through town.

	Col. 40
No	0
Yes	1
Don't know; it depends	7
NA	9

89. Take indirect actions such as picketing or boycotting or petitioning.

	Col. 41
No	0
Yes	1
Don't know; it depends	7
NA	9

90. Take direct actions such as strikes or "sit-ins" or "walk-outs."

	Col. 42
No	0
Yes	1
Don't know; it depends	7
NA	9

91. Stage mass protest demonstrations with large crowds of people.

	Col. 43
No	0
Yes	1
Don't know; it depends	7
NA	9

92. Engage in civil disobedience by purposefully breaking minor laws.

	Col. 44
No	0
Yes	1
Don't know; it depends	7
NA	9

93. Take part in riots and rebellions.

	Col. 45
No	0
Yes	1
Don't know; it depends	7
NA	9

Finally, the last few questions deal with your job as a parole officer aide. First:

94. What do you consider to be your main job as a Parole Officer Aide?   Col. 46

95. How much education is necessary for a Parole Officer Aide to function well? (high school, college, etc.)   Col. 47

96. Is the quality of being a community resident located in the same general area as most of the parolees on your caseload more or less important than the quality of being an ex-offender?   Col. 48

97. What helps you the most—knowing the community and its contacts, or having the life experience of an ex-offender?   Col. 49

98. You are limited in your powers to arrest—does this help or hinder your effectiveness?   Col. 50

    How and why?   Col. 51

99. Is establishing a good relationship with your supervisor a key issue in your success?   Col. 52

    Why or why not?   Col. 53

100. Have you experienced any resentment or jealousy toward you from the other parole officers since you came on the job?   Cols. 54-55

     If yes, what or how?

101. As you undoubtedly know, you do not make as much money as the other parole officers. How do you feel about this?   Col. 56

102. Do you feel you are really helping the "ex-con" from the position of his parole officer, or could you help more another way?   Col. 57

103. According to the design of the program (particularly your limitations on authority and caseloads), do you feel you are more or less effective than the average parole officer? Why?   Cols. 58-59

104. What problems do you encounter that the average parole officer does not?   Col. 60

105. What are your feelings about being given ten "multi-problem" cases from other parole officers' caseloads? Were they taking unfair advantage, given the "dirty work," or was it a challenge, a chance to prove yourself?   Col. 61

106. What changes would you make in the program according to:

    A.   Selection of POAs   Col. 62

    B.   Training of POAs   Col. 63

    C.   Supervision of POAs   Col. 64

    D.   Administration of the program   Col. 65

107. How is the POA program received in the community by: Col. 66

    Police

    Employers

    Churches

    Neighbors

    Families

    Friends

    Others (who)

108. What are your criticisms, positive and negative comments about the training session?   Col. 67

109. Have they been of any help?   Col. 68

110. Should they have been more extensive?   Col. 69

111. Did you really learn anything?   Col. 70

112. If you were in charge of the next training session for aides, what would you do differently?   Col. 71

113. Have you experienced any problems in your work due to your age or race? If so, how have you handled them?   Col. 72

114. Race of Respondent (Record after interview is over)

	Col. 73
White	0
Black	1
DK	9

Do you have any additional comments about your job, the POA Program or this interview?

Students' Guidelines for Field Interviews with Parole Officers and Parole Officer Aides

Name: _____

Date: _____

City: _____

Parole Officer: _____

Interview

We want you to keep track of the day's events by making notes on 3x5 cards. *Remember*—record data only when away from parole officers and parolees. Your task is to make observations without causing undue nervousness.

After your trip, make a 1 - 2 page summary to hand in with this paper using the following guidelines:

1. How many parolees were seen during the day?
    a. Where were they seen; for how long?
    b. Reason for contact?
    c. When was last contact between PO & parolee?

2. An estimate of time spent in each of the following:
    a. with parolees
    b. traveling
    c. writing reports or recording data
    d. staff or other meetings (specify)
    e. anything else (specify)
    Give percentages and some narrative.

3. Describe anything else done during the day having relevance; give your reactions and comments to anything you feel is important to note.

4. How well do you feel your parole officer got along with the parolees on his caseload?

    Excellent Good Satisfactory Less than satisfactory Very poor

    Why? _____

    _____

5. How well do you feel your parole officer got along with fellow staff members?

Excellent   Good   Satisfactory   Less than satisfactory   Very poor

Why? _____

_____

Release-from-Legal-Responsibility Forms for Students

State of Ohio
Department of Rehabilitation
and Correction

Adult Parole Authority
1050 Freeway Drive North
Columbus, Ohio 43229

Release from Legal Responsibility

Please Print Information

Date: _____

I, _____ ,

(Name: last,   first   middle or maiden)

do hereby release the Adult Parole Authority from all legal responsibility and liability for any accident or injury which I might suffer or receive during my association with the Adult Parole Authority while serving as a

_____

(title of position: student trainee, student intern, volunteer worker, etc.)

Furthermore, I do hereby agree to respect the confidentiality of all Adult Parole Authority records to which I may be granted access and of all private interviews or counseling sessions in which I may take part.

Signature: _____

(full legal name)

Signature of
Parent or
Guardian*: _____

(full legal name)
*(Required if person is a legal minor)

Witnessed: Name _____

Title _____

Date _____

161

The Interview Form for Supervisors

Employee _____

Three characteristics often mentioned as necessary for a parole officer to perform well on his job are:

1. The ability to motivate parolees.
2. The ability to relate in a non-threatening and yet firm manner with parolees.
3. The ability to put himself out, or in other words go the extra mile, in working with parolees.

Now we would like you to evaluate _____
with regards to each of the above characteristics. The average score on each of these characteristics is 50. First, how well does he motivate the parolees he works with?

       Poor   Average   Excellent
1. Motivate
   0 10 20 30 40 50 60 70 80 90 100

       Poor   Average   Excellent
2. Relate
   0 10 20 30 40 50 60 70 80 90 100

       Poor   Average   Excellent
3. Put Out
   0 10 20 30 40 50 60 70 80 90 100

4. Which one of the following statements best describes what value _____ _____ is to the APA?

____1. He could fill immediately a specific job at higher management level, no further training necessary. (immediately promotable)

____2. He could fill a specific job at a higher management level with further training. (promotable)

____3. He is doing what can reasonably be expected of him on his present level. (satisfactory plus)

____4. He is doing what can reasonably be expected on his present job but he is not seen as going beyond his present level in the immediate future. (satisfactory)

Employee _____

____5. His performance on his present assignment is not completely satis-
factory. (questionable)

____6. His performance is not acceptable on his present job. He may be able to
improve his performance with further help and encouragement. (unsatis-
factory)

5. Now using the same grading system we used earlier, how would you rate __
_____ with other officers you know at getting jobs or special job training
for parolees?

      Poor   Average   Excellent

Jobs

  0 10 20 30 40 50 60 70 80 90 100

• 6. How would you rate _____ in relating and getting along with fellow
workers?

      Poor   Average   Excellent

Relating colleagues

  0 10 20 30 40 50 60 70 80 90 100

7. How would you rate_____ in relating and getting along with
representatives of other programs and agencies in the community?

      Poor   Average   Excellent

Relating community

  0 10 20 30 40 50 60 70 80 90 100

8. How would you rate _____'s report writing?

      Poor   Average   Excellent

Report writing

  0 10 20 30 40 50 60 70 80 90 100

Comment:

9. How would you rate _____ overall as an employee of the APA?

      Poor   Average   Excellent

Overall

  0 10 20 30 40 50 60 70 80 90 100

Employee _____

10. Approximately how many times has_____ spoken as a representative of the APA (i.e. community gatherings, schools, clubs) since his employment.

[Get an estimate]

11. How valuable a function is this?

12. Is there anything _____ has been doing that others generally do not do in your office?

13. We would now like to ask you some specific questions about the Parole Officer Aid Program. First, what, if any, are its advantages?

14. What are its disadvantages?

15. If you were responsible for evaluating and restructuring the program, what would you do? (Probe)

The Inmate Questionnaire

This study is being conducted by the Program for the Study of Crime and Delinquency at the Ohio State University. We are conducting this survey to find out how you feel about a program presently operating in Ohio. The program involves the use of ex-offenders as parole officer aides. Your cooperation on this survey will help us to have a better understanding of this program. Your opinion will also help us get an idea of how inmates feel about the services they may get while on parole. Nobody from the Division of Corrections, the Adult Parole Authority, or this prison will be allowed to see your answers. The only people who will see your answers are staff members of the Research Center at The Ohio State University.

This is not a test. There are no wrong or right answers. Your answers will be combined with those of many other inmates and examined as a group. Please answer all of the questions as honestly as you can.

Date: _____

Directions: Please read each question and circle the answer you wish to make.

1. The State of Ohio has recently hired a number of "ex-cons" to work as parole officers (or parole officer aides). If you had your choice, when released from prison, would you prefer:

   An "ex-con" as a PO   A normal PO (not an "ex-con")

2. Do you believe the idea of hiring "ex-cons" as parole officers is:

   A good idea   A bad idea   Not good or bad

3. In what ways do you think an "ex-con" working as a parole officer, might be *better* than a regular parole officer? (Please list *every way* in which you think an "ex-con" might be a better parole officer.)

4. In what ways might an "ex-con" be *worse* than a non "ex-con" as a parole officer? (Please list *every way* in which you think an "ex-con" might make a *worse* parole officer.)

5. Did you know about the state's program of hiring "ex-cons" to work as parole officers *before* filling out this questionnaire?

   Yes   No

Now we have some additional questions about the parole department's program of using "ex-cons" as parole officers. *There are no right or wrong answers.* We want you to tell us how you feel about each of these statements by circling the answer you prefer.

6. It will be easier for an "ex-con" parole officer to help parolees avoid problems than is now the case with normal parole officers.

   Strongly disagree   Disagree   Undecided   Agree   Strongly agree

7. Parolees who have an "ex-con" as their parole officer are more likely to succeed on parole than those who do not.

   Strongly disagree   Disagree   Undecided   Agree   Strongly agree

8. Most parolees will object to being supervised by an "ex-con" parole officer rather than a normal parole officer.

   Strongly disagree   Disagree   Undecided   Agree   Strongly agree

9. Most parole officers now find it hard to understand parolees' problems because the officers come from middle-class backgrounds.

   Strongly disagree   Disagree   Undecided   Agree   Strongly agree

10. The use of "ex-cons" as parole officers will probably result in new treatment programs for helping parolees stay out of jail and prison.

   Strongly disagree   Disagree   Undecided   Agree   Strongly agree

11. Following release from prison and completion of parole, I would like to become a parole officer if given the chance.

   Strongly disagree   Disagree   Undecided   Agree   Strongly agree

12. Race should make no difference in how well a parole officer does his job.

   Strongly disagree   Disagree   Undecided   Agree   Strongly agree

13. On your last birthday, how old were you?

   _____

14. What is your race?

   Black   White   Other

15. How many years of school have you completed?_____ years completed
   _____ grade completed

16. How many times in your life have you been arrested?

   _____

17. How old were you when you were first arrested?

   _____

18. How old were you the first time you were sent to any correctional institution (training school, boys' school, reform school, prison, road camp, etc.)?

_____

19. How much time have you spent *altogether* in your life so far at correctional institutions (training school, boys' school, reform school, prison, road camp, etc.)?

_____ months?

20. Have you ever been on parole?

        Yes   No

21. When you leave this institution will you be on parole?

        Yes   No

22. Do you think it is a good idea to release inmates on parole?

        Yes   No

23. Do you think it would be better to simply have judges give defendants definite sentences and do away with parole boards and parole?

        Yes   No

24. Do you think future employers will hold your being an "ex-con" against you?

        Yes   No

25. What institution are you now in?

A. Ohio Penitentiary   1
B. Ohio State Reformatory at Mansfield   2
C. London Correctional Institution   3
D. Chillicothe Correctional Institution   4
E. Marion Correctional Institution   5
F. Lebanon Correctional Institution   6
G. Marysville Reformatory   7
H. Lucasville   8

The Parolee Questionnaire

Directions: Circle your answer. ◯

1. How old are you? _____

2. Race:

    White   Black   Other

3. Are you presently employed or in a job-training program?

    Yes   No

4. What is the highest grade of school you have completed?

    8 years or less   9-11 years   12 years or more

5. What is your average income *per week*?

    $75 or less $76-$125 $126 or more

6. How many months were you in prison (reformatory or correctional institution) this last time?

    months: _____

Now we would like some specific information about your parole officer (or parole officer aide).

7. Can you communicate well with your parole officer? (Do you and he speak the same language?)

    Yes   No

8. Do you trust your parole officer?

    Yes   No

9. Does he listen to you and seem to care about what you say and do?

    Yes   No

10. How often do you "con" your PO?

    Often   Sometimes   Never

11. Would your PO "go the extra mile," or do more than is necessary for you?

    Yes   No

12. Does your PO have connections he uses to help get you jobs?

    Yes   No

13. Does your PO really understand what it is like to be on parole?

    Yes   No

14. How often do you have contact with your PO (see him or talk to him on the phone)?

More than once a week	Once a week	Once a month	Twice a month	Once a month	Less than once a month

15. Is your PO easy to find if you need to see him or talk to him?

    Yes   No

16. If you commit a parole violation, would your PO give you a second chance?

    Yes   No   Don't know

17. Would your PO rather see you "make it" in your community or send you back to an institution?

    See you "make it"   Send you back   Don't know

18. Are you required to visit your PO at his office, or does he come to your job or home to visit you?

    Visit required at his office   He finds me

19. Do other parolees assigned to your PO feel he is doing a good job?

    Yes   No   Don't know

20. How would you rate your PO's ability to motivate parolees?

0   10   20   30   40   50   60   70   80   90   100
  Poor   Average   Excellent

21. How would you rate his ability to get along with you and help you?

0   10   20   30   40   50   60   70   80   90   100
  Poor   Average   Excellent

22. How would you rate your PO in putting himself out or going the extra mile in helping parolees?

0   10   20   30   40   50   60   70   80   90   100
  Poor   Average   Excellent

23. How would you rate him overall as a parole officer?

0   10   20   30   40   50   60   70   80   90   100
  Poor   Average   Excellent

24. When were you released from prison? _____
                                     month   year

25. If you had your choice would you want a parole officer or a parole officer aide to supervise you on parole?

     Parole Officer   Parole Officer Aide

26. Have you found employers hold your being an "ex-con" against you?

        Yes   No

27. Have the police questioned you about any crime since your release from prison?

        Yes   No

28. Have the police picked you up or arrested you since your release from prison?

        Yes   No

29. Have you been to court for a new offense (except traffic) since your release from prison?

    Yes   No

30. Have you spent time in jail since your release from prison?

    Yes   No

31. How could your PO do a better job?

   _____

   _____

Letter to Parolees

Name
Address
City, State

Dear Mr.

The Program for the Study of Crime and Delinquency of Ohio State University is conducting a scientific survey to find out how parolees feel about parole conditions and about their parole officer (or parole officer aide). Your help will give us an idea of how parolees feel about the services they get while on parole. Nobody from the Division of Corrections or the Adult Parole Authority will be allowed to see your answers. The only persons who will see your answers are the research staff at Ohio State University.

I am writing to ask for your help in this study. In order to get all kinds of parolees, parole officers or aides were picked first. Next, a group of men who had been or were on their case load was chosen. You were chosen in this way. We hope very much you will take a few minutes to fill out this questionnaire. You have the promise of the director of this study that no one in the Department of Corrections or the Adult Parole Authority will ever see your questionnaire. The information is confidential. No names are used in our report writing and you will *not* get into trouble as a result of your answers.

There are no right or wrong answers. We only want to know what you think about each question. Your answers will be combined with those of other parolees and looked at only as a group. Answer all of the questions to the best of your ability and please be honest.

The first page of this survey is for you to give the researchers some information about yourself. On the other pages, you will be asked to circle the answer that best shows the way you feel about a statement.

If you would like further information about the Program for the Study of Crime and Delinquency or this study, I would be happy to answer any questions. Thank you for your help.

Yours truly,

Dr. Joseph E. Scott, Associate
Program for the Study of Crime
and Delinquency
206-210

JES:mh
Encl.

The National Survey
Questionnaire

1. Is your state utilizing ex-offenders in the correctional system as:

    Parole officer aides
    $\overline{}$ $\overline{}$
    Yes   No

    Probation officer aides
    $\overline{}$ $\overline{}$
    Yes   No

    Others (specify)_____

2. If your state is utilizing ex-offenders, please answer items 3 through 15. If not, proceed to item 16.

3. When did the program begin?

    Parole officer aides
    _____
    Date

    Probation officer aides
    _____
    Date

    Others (specify)_____
    _____
    Date

4. Are your aides:

    Volunteers
    $\overline{}$ $\overline{}$
    Yes   No

    Paid staff members
    $\overline{}$ $\overline{}$
    Yes   No

    Others (specify) _____

5. How many ex-offenders is your program authorized to employ?

    Parole officer aides
    _____

    Probation officer aides
    _____

    Others (specify) _____
    _____

6. How many ex-offenders does your program actually employ?

    Parole officer aides
    _____

6. (cont.)

       Probation officer aides   _____

       Others (specify) _____   _____

7. What is the annual budget for the program?

       Parole officer aides $ _____

       Probation officer aides $ _____

       Others (specify) _____ $ _____

8. In the space below, indicate source of funding (e.g., NIMH, LEAA, Ford Foundation):

9. What is the beginning annual salary for:

       Parole officer aides $ _____

       Probation officer aides $ _____

       Others (specify) _____ $ _____

10. On the following scale, rate the *overall job performance* of aides in relation to regular staff members performing similar tasks. Circle the appropriate number:

	Poor	Average	Excellent
Parole officer aide	0 10 20 30 40 50 60 70 80 90 100		
Probation officer aide	0 10 20 30 40 50 60 70 80 90 100		
Others (specify)_____	0 10 20 30 40 50 60 70 80 90 100		

11. What is the maximum annual salary for:

       Parole officer aides $ _____

       Probation officer aides $ _____

Others (specify) _____   _____

12. Do aides have release time from the job for educational advancement?

Yes   No

13. Do aides have financial aid for educational advancement?

Yes   No

14. If answer to item 13 is "yes," what is the source of the funding?

15. Below, briefly describe the criteria used in selecting ex-offenders to be employed as aides:

16. Are there legal restrictions in your state prohibiting the employment of ex-offenders as parole/probation officer aides?

Yes   No

17. If the answer to item 16 is "yes," briefly describe such restraints below:

18. Are there policy or administrative restraints in your state preventing the employment of ex-offenders as parole/probation officer aides?

Yes   No

19. If the answer to item 18 is "yes," briefly describe such restraints below:

20. What is your opinion as to the desirability of utilizing ex-offenders as parole/probation officer aides? Circle the appropriate response:

Very undesirable   Undesirable   Desirable   Very desirable

21. In the space below, briefly indicate the major advantages to utilizing ex-offenders as parole/probation officer aides:

22. In the space below, briefly indicate the major disadvantages to utilizing ex-offenders as parole/probation officer aides:

23. If you would like to receive the results of this survey, please indicate by a check in this space: _____

Letter to State Directors

March 11, 1974

Dear Sir:

At the Program for the Study of Crime and Delinquency, we are in the process of evaluating a program in Ohio using ex-offenders as parole officer aides. In attempting to analyze the results of this program it would be most helpful to have something to compare against. The National Advisory Commission on Criminal Justice has recommended that states explore the possible use of ex-offenders in corrections. The National Council on Crime and Delinquency in 1965 surveyed the fifty states' use of ex-offenders but since that time, nationwide, no data has been gathered on the subject.

We are asking you to complete the enclosed questionnaire. The questions are brief and we wish to make minimal demands upon your time. Return the questionnaire in the accompanying envelope. A space has been provided in the last item of the questionnaire for you to check if you wish to receive a copy of the results of the survey.

We greatly appreciate your cooperation.

Thank you,

Joseph E. Scott, Ph.D.
Professor, Sociology

Notes

Notes

Chapter 1
Background and Development of the
Use of Paraprofessionals

1. Jewel Goddard and Gerald D. Jacobson, "Volunteer Services in a Juvenile Court," *Crime and Delinquency*, vol. 13 (April 1967), pp. 337-43.

2. Alan Gartner, *Paraprofessionals and Their Performance: A Survey of Education, Health, and Social Service Programs* (New York, Praeger Publishers, 1971).

3. Robert Reiff and Frank Riessman, *The Indigenous Non-Professional, A Strategy of Change in Community Action and Community Mental Health Programs* (New York: Monograph Series, Number 1, Behavioral Publications, Inc., 1965), p. 7, fourth printing (1970).

4. Robert R. Carkhuff, *Helping and Human Relations: A Primer for Lay and Professional Helpers*, vol. 1 (New York: Holt Rinehart and Winston Inc., 1969).

Robert R. Carkhuff and C.B. Truax, "Lay Mental Health Counseling: The Effects of Lay Group Counseling," *Journal of Consulting Psychology*, vol. 29, 1965, pp. 426-32.

G. Banks, B.G. Berenson, and R.R. Carkhuff, "The Effects of Counselor Race and Training Upon Negro Clients in Initial Interviews," *Journal of Clinical Psychology*, vol. 23, 1967, pp. 70-72.

5. Frank Riessman, *The Revolution in Social Work: The New Nonprofessional* (New York: Mobilization for Youth, 1963).

6. Aaron Schmais, *Implementing Nonprofessional Programs in Human Services* (New York: Graduate School of Social Work, New York University, 1967), p. 6.

7. Arthur Pearl and Frank Riessman, *New Careers for the Poor: The Nonprofessional in Human Service* (New York: The Free Press, 1965).

8. J. McKee, "Reinforcement Theory and the Convict Culture," *American Correctional Association Proceedings*, 1964, pp. 175-76.

9. "Prison Days and Nights at MCI Walpole," *The Mentor* (july 1969). Published by the inmates of Massachusetts Correctional Institution, Walpole, Mass.

10. J.E. Baker, "Inmate of Self Government," *Journal of Criminal Law, Criminology and Police Science*, vol. 55 (March 1964), pp. 39-47.

11. Albert Morris, "The Involvement of Offenders in the Prevention and Correction of Criminal Behavior," Bulletin No. 20, Boston, Mass.: Massachusetts Correctional Association (October 1970), pp. 6-7.

12. Paul Keve, *Imaginative Programming in Probation and Parole*, University of Minnesota Press, 1967, p. 212.

13. Ibid., p. 216.

14. Albert Morris, op. cit.

15. Edward Sagarin, *Odd Man In: Societies of Deviants in America* (Chicago: Quadrangle Books, 1969).

16. Billy Sands, *The Seventh Step* (New York: New American Library, 1967).

17. EFEC (Efforts From Ex-Convicts), "Statement of Purpose," Washington, D.C., 1966.

18. "Street Christians: Jesus as the Ultimate Trip," *Time Magazine* (August 3, 1970), pp. 31-32.

19. Los Angeles Police Department, "An Interim Evaluation of the Community Relations Aides' Performance in the Community Relations Program," Los Angeles, Calif., 1969.

20. LaMar Empey, "Offender Participation in the Correctional Process: General Theoretical Issues," *Offenders as a Correctional Manpower Resource*, Joint Commission on Correctional Manpower and Training, Washington, D.C., p. 6.

21. Raymond D. Clements, *Paraprofessionals in Probation and Parole: A Manual for Their Selection Training Induction and Supervision in Day to Day Tasks* (Chicago: University of Chicago, 1972).

22. "Offenders as a Correctional Manpower Resource," Joint Commission on Correctional Manpower and Training, Washington, D.C., 1968, pp. 88-90.

23. Albert Morris, op. cit.

24. Intercom Staff Writer, "Growing People and Their Skills," *Intercom*, vol. 10, 1969.

25. "New Careers Development Project, Final Report," National Institute of Mental Health Project (OM-01616), sponsored by the Institute for the Study of Crime and Delinquency, September 1964-August 1967.

26. W.S. Pilcher, D.W. Beless, and E.R. Rest, *Probation Officer Case Aid Project, Final Report, Phase I* (September 1971), Center for Studies in Criminal Justice, University of Chicago Law School.

W.S. Pilcher, G. Witkowski, E.R. Rest, and G.J. Busiel, *Probation Officer Case Aid Project, Final Report*, Phase II (September 1972), Center for Studies in Criminal Justice, University of Chicago Law School.

27. Alan B. Chandler and Allen Lee, "Final Report for Project MOST," Oregon State Corrections Division (March 1972).

28. A. Pearl and F. Riessman, op. cit.

29. F. Riessman, "The 'Helper' Therapy Principle," *Social Work*, vol. 10 (April 1965), p. 28.

30. Rita Volkman and Donald R. Cressey, "Differential Association and the Rehabilitation of Drug Addicts," *American Journal of Sociology*, vol. 69 (September 1963), p. 139.

31. Charles Grosser, et al., "Manpower Development Programs," chapter 8, *Nonprofessionals in the Human Services* (San Francisco: Jossey-Bass, Inc., 1969).

Chapter 2
The Parole Officer Aide Program
in Ohio

1. Nick Sanborn, "Summary of Progress and Operational Guidelines: Report on the Use of the Ex-Offender as a Parole Officer Aide" (unpublished), 1972.

Chapter 3
Methodology

1. Allen L. Edwards, *The Edwards Personal Preference Schedule* (New York: Psychological Corporation, 1959). *See also* Henry A. Murray, *Explorations in Personality* (New York: Oxford University Press, 1938). Desmond S. Cartwright and Richard J. Robertson, "Membership in Cliques and Achievement," *American Journal of Sociology*, vol. 66 (March 1961), pp. 441-45.

2. Morris Rosenberg, "The Association between Self-Esteem and Anxiety," *Journal of Psychiatric Research*, vol. 1, 1962, pp. 135-52.

3. Leo Srole, "Social Integration and Certain Corollaries: An Exploratory Study," *American Sociological Review*, vol. 21 (December 1956), pp. 709-16.

4. Arthur Neal, "Stratification Concommitants of Powerlessness and Normlessness: A Study of Political and Economic Alienation," unpublished Ph.D. dissertation, Ohio State University. *See also* Arthur Neal and Solomon Rettig, "Dimensions of Alienation Among Manual and Non-Manual Workers," *American Sociological Review*, vol. 69 (November 1959), pp. 270-84.

5. Herbert McClosky, "Conservatism and Personality," *American Political Science Review*, vol. 52 (March 1958), pp. 27-45.

6. Verling C. Troldahl and Fredric A. Powell, "A Short-Form Dogmatism Scale For Use In Field Studies," *Social Forces*, vol. 44 (December 1965), pp. 211-14.

7. Rolf H.K. Schulze, "A Shortened Version of the Rokeach Dogmatism Scale," *Journal of Psychological Studies*, vol. 13, 1962, pp. 93-97.

8. Joseph E. Scott, "The Use of Discretion in Determining the Severity of Punishment for Incarcerated Offenders," *The Journal of Criminal Law and Criminology*, vol. 74, no. 2, 1974, pp. 214-24. A detailed explanation of how prior criminal involvement was computed is given on pp. 216-217.

Chapter 4
Attitudes and Orientations of Parole
Officer in Comparison to Aides

1. Henry A. Murray (ed.), *Explorations in Personality* (New York: Oxford University Press, 1938), p. 164.

2. Marian Winterbottom, "The Relation of Need for Achievement to Learning Experiences in Independence and Mastery," *Motives in Fantasy, Action and Society* (Princeton, N.J.: D. Van Nortrand Press, 1958), pp. 453-78.

3. Herbert J. Goldings, "On the Avowal and Projection of Happiness," *Journal of Personality*, vol. 23, 1954, pp. 30-47.

4. Walter B. Miller, "Lower Class Culture as a Generating Milieu of Gang Delinquency," *Journal of Social Issues*, vol. 14, 1958, pp. 5-19.

5. Leo Srole, "Social Integration and Certain Corollaries: An Exploratory Study," *American Sociological Review*, vol. 21, 1956, pp. 709-16.

6. Wendell Bell, "Anomie, Social Isolation and the Class Structure," *Sociometry*, vol. 20, 1957, pp. 105-16.

7. Julian B. Rotter, Melvin Seeman, and Shephard Liverant, "Internal vs. External Control of Reinforcements: A Major Variable in Behavior Theory," *Decisions, Values and Groups*, vol. 2, (London: Pergamon Press, 1962), p. 499.

8. Ibid., pp. 473-516.

9. Milton Rokeach, *The Open and Closed Mind* (New York: Basic Books, 1960), p. 71.

10. Ibid., p. 4.

11. A.H. Hastorf, and I.E. Bender, "A Caution Respecting the Measurement of Empathic Ability," *Journal of Abnormal and Social Psychology*, vol. 47, 1952, pp. 574-76.

12. Charles W. Hobart, and Nancy Fahlberg, "The Measurement of Empathy," *American Journal of Sociology*, vol. 70, 1965, pp. 595-603.

Chapter 5
The Findings: Data on Supervisors',
Inmates', and Parolees' Attitudes
Concerning Parole Officer Aides

1. James Robinson and Gerald Smith, "The Effectiveness of Correctional Programs," *Crime and Delinquency* (January 1971), pp. 67-80.

2. Gene Kassebaum, David A. Ward, and Daniel M. Wilner, *Prison Treatment and Parole Survival: An Empirical Assessment* (New York: John Wiley & Sons, Inc., 1971).

3. Robert M. Martinson, "Correctional Treatment: An Empirical Assessment," unpublished manuscript.

Chapter 6
National Survey of States' Use of
Ex-Offenders in Parole and Probation Work

1. "Offenders as a Correctional Manpower Resource," Joint Commission on Correctional Manpower and Training, Washington, D.C., 1968.

2. "Corrections," National Advisory Commission on Criminal Justice Standards and Goals, Washington, D.C., 1973, pp. 478-79.

3. Thomas J. Callanan, "The Ex-Offender as Paraprofessional in a Correctional Setting," *Corrections: Problems of Punishment and Rehabilitation*, edited by Edward Sagarin and Donal E.J. MacNamara (New York: Praeger Publishers, 1973).

4. James W. Hunt, James Bowers, and Neal Miller, *Laws, Licenses and the Offender's Right to Work* (Washington, D.C.: National Clearinghouse on Offender Employment Restrictions and The American Bar Association, 1973).

5. "Offenders as a Correctional Manpower Resource."

6. Gilbert Geis, "Laws, Politics, and Ex-Offender in the Correctional Process," in ibid., pp. 22-30.

Bibliography

Bibliography

Baker, J.E. "Inmate of Self Government." *Journal of Criminal Law, Criminology and Police Science*, vol. 55 (March 1964), pp. 39-47.

Banks, G., B.G. Berenson, and R.R. Carkhuff. "The Effects of Counselor Race and Training Upon Negro Clients In Initial Interviews," *Journal of Clinical Psychology*, vol. 23 (1967), pp. 70-72.

Bell, Wendell. "Anomie, Social Isolation, and the Class Structure," *Sociometry*, vol. 20 (1957), pp. 105-16.

Callanan, Thomas J. "The Ex-Offender as Paraprofessional in a Correctional Setting." *Corrections: Problems of Punishment and Rehabilitation.* Edited by Edward Sagarin and Donal E.J. MacNamara. New York: Praeger Publishers, 1973.

Carkhuff, Robert R. *Helping and Human Relations: A Primer for Lay and Professional Helpers*, vol. 1. New York: Holt, Rinehart and Winston, Inc., 1969.

Carkhuff, Robert R., and C.B. Truax. "Lay Mental Health Counseling: The Effects of Lay Group Counseling," *Journal of Consulting Psychology*, vol. 29 (1965), pp. 426-32.

Cartwright, Desmond S., and Richard J. Robertson. "Membership in Cliques and Achievement," *American Journal of Sociology*, vol. 66 (March 1961), pp. 441-45.

Chandler, Alan B., and Allen Lee. "Final Report for Project MOST," Oregon State Corrections Division, March 1972.

Clements, Raymond D. *Paraprofessionals in Probation and Parole: A Manual for Their Selection, Training, Induction and Supervision in Day to Day Tasks.* Chicago: University of Chicago, 1972.

Corrections. Washington, D.C.: National Advisory Commission on Criminal Justice Standards and Goals, 1973.

Edwards, Allen L. *The Edwards Personal Preference Schedule.* New York: Psychological Corporation, 1959.

EFEC (Efforts From Ex-Convicts). "Statement of Purpose." Washington, D.C., 1966.

Empey, LaMar. "Offender Participation in the Correctional Process: General Theoretical Issues." *Offenders as a Correctional Manpower Resource.* Washington, D.C.: Joint Commission on Correctional Manpower and Training, 1968.

Gartner, Alan. *Paraprofessionals and Their Performance: A Survey of Education, Health, and Social Service Programs.* New York: Praeger Publishers, 1971.

Geis, Gilbert. "Law, Politics, and Ex-Offenders in the Correctional Process." *Offenders as a Correctional Manpower Resource.* Washington, D.C.: Joint Commission on Correctional Manpower and Training, 1968.

Goddard, Jewel, and Gerald D. Jacobson. "Volunteer Services in a Juvenile Court," *Crime and Delinquency*, vol. 13 (April 1967), pp. 337-43.

Goldings, Herbert J. "On the Avowal and Projection of Happiness," *Journal of Personality*, vol. 23 (1954), pp. 30-47.

Grosser, Charles, et al. "Manpower Development Programs," chapter 8, *Nonprofessionals in the Human Services*. San Francisco: Jossey-Bass, Inc., 1969.

Hastorf, A.H., and I.E. Bender. "A Caution Respecting the Measurement of Empathic Ability," *Journal of Abnormal and Social Psychology*, vol. 47 (1952), pp. 574-76.

Hobart, Charles W., and Nancy Fahlberg. "The Measurement of Empathy," *American Journal of Sociology*, vol. 70 (1965), pp. 595-603.

Hunt, James W., James Bowers, and Neal Miller. *Laws, Licenses and the Offender's Right to Work*. Washington, D.C.: National Clearinghouse on Offender Employment Restrictions and The American Bar Association, 1973.

Intercom Staff Writer. "Growing People and Their Skills," *Intercom*, vol. 10 (1969).

Kassebaum, Gene, David A. Ward, and Daniel M. Wilner. *Prison Treatment and Parole Survival: An Empirical Assessment*. New York: John Wiley & Sons, Inc.

Keve, Paul. *Imaginative Programming in Probation and Parole*. University of Minnesota Press, 1967.

Los Angeles Police Department. "An Interim Evaluation of the Community Relations Aides' Performance in the Community Relations Program." Los Angeles, 1969.

McClosky, Herbert. "Conservatism and Personality," *American Political Science Review*, vol. 52 (March 1958), pp. 27-45.

McKee, J. "Reinforcement Theory and the Convict Culture," *American Correctional Association Proceedings*, (1964), pp. 175-76.

Martinson, Robert M. "Correctional Treatment: An Empirical Assessment," unpublished manuscript.

Miller, Walter B. "Lower Class Culture as a Generating Milieu of Gang Delinquency," *Journal of Social Issues*, vol. 14 (1958), pp. 5-19.

Morris, Albert. "The Involvement of Offenders in the Prevention and Correction of Criminal Behavior," Bulletin No. 20. Boston: Massachusetts Correctional Association, October 1970.

Murray, Henry A., ed. *Explorations in Personality*. New York: Oxford University Press, 1938.

Neal, Arthur, and Solomon Rettig. "Dimensions of Alienation Among Manual and Non-Manual Workers," *American Sociological Review*, vol. 69 (November 1959), pp. 270-84.

Neal, Arthur. "Stratification Concomitants of Powerlessness and Normlessness: A Study of Political and Economic Alienation." Unpublished Ph.D. dissertation, Ohio State University.

"New Careers Development Project, Final Report." National Institute of Mental Health Project (OM-01616), Sponsored by the Institute for the Study of Crime and Delinquency, September 1964-August 1967.

Offenders as a Correctional Manpower Resource. Washington, D.C.: Joint Commission on Correctional Manpower and Training, 1968.

Pearl, Arthur, and Frank Riessman. *New Careers for the Poor: The Nonprofessional in Human Service.* New York: The Free Press, 1965.

Pilcher, W.S., D.W. Beless, and E.R. Rest. *Probation Officer Case Aid Project, Final Report, Phase I.* Center for Studies in Criminal Justice, University of Chicago Law School, September 1971.

Pilcher, W.S., G. Witkowski, E.R. Rest, and G.J. Busiel. *Probation Officer Case Aid Project, Final Report, Phase II.* Center for Studies in Criminal Justice, University of Chicago Law School, September 1972.

"Prison Days and Nights at MCI Walpole," *The Mentor*, July 1969. Published by the inmates of the Massachusetts Correctional Institution, Walpole, Massachusetts.

Reiff, Robert, and Frank Riessman. *The Indigenous Non-Professional, A Strategy of Change in Community Action and Community Mental Health Programs.* Monograph Series, Number 1. New York: Behavioral Publications, Inc., 1965.

Riessman, Frank. "The 'Helper' Therapy Principle," *Social Work*, vol. 10 (April 1965).

Riessman, Frank. *The Revolution in Social Work: The New Nonprofessional.* New York: Mobilization for Youth, 1963.

Robinson, James, and Gerald Smith. "The Effectiveness of Correctional Programs," *Crime and Delinquency* (January 1971), pp. 67-80.

Rokeach, Milton. *The Open and Closed Mind.* New York: Basic Books, 1960.

Rosenberg, Morris. "The Association between Self-Esteem and Anxiety," *Journal of Psychiatric Research*, vol. 1 (1962), pp. 135-52.

Rotter, Julian B., Melvin Seeman, and Shepard Liverant. "Internal vs. External Control of Reinforcements: A Major Variable in Behavior Theory," *Decisions, Values and Groups*, vol. 2. London: Pergamon Press, 1962.

Sagarin, Edward. *Odd Man In: Societies of Deviants in America.* Chicago: Quadrangle Books, 1969.

Sanborn, Nick. "Summary of Progress and Operational Guidelines: Report on the Use of the Ex-Offender as a Parole Officer Aide." Unpublished, 1972.

Sands, Billy. *The Seventh Step.* New York: New American Library, 1967.

Schmais, Aaron. *Implementing Nonprofessional Programs in Human Services.* New York: Graduate School of Social Work, New York University, 1967.

Schulze, Rolf H.K. "A Shortened Version of the Rokeach Dogmatism Scale," *Journal of Psychological Studies*, vol. 13 (1962), pp. 93-97.

Srole, Leo. "Social Integration and Certain Corollaries: An Exploratory Study," *American Sociological Review*, vol. 21 (December 1956), pp. 709-16.

"Street Christians: Jesus as the Ultimate Trip," *Time Magazine* (August 3, 1970), pp. 31-32.

Trodahl, Verling C., and Fredric A. Powell. "A Short-Form Dogmatism Scale for Use in Field Studies," *Social Forces*, vol. 44 (December 1965), pp. 211-14.

Volkman, Rita, and Donald R. Cressey. "Differential Association and the Rehabilitation of Drug Addicts," *American Journal of Sociology*, vol. 69 (September 1963), pp. 138-42.

Winterbottom, Marian. "The Relation of Need for Achievement to Learning Experience in Independence and Mastery." *Motives in Fantasy, Action and Society*. Princeton, New Jersey: D. Van Nostrand Press, 1958.

Index

Index

About the Author

Joseph E. Scott is assistant professor of sociology and associate at the Center for the Study of Crime and Delinquency, The Ohio State University. He received the Ph.D. in sociology from Indiana University in 1972. Professor Scott's research interests focus on radical alternatives to prison; he has also done extensive research on parole board decision-making and shock-parole. In addition, he completed a major cross cultural research project on white collar crime, punishment, and criminal justice systems in Scandinavia, the Netherlands, and Great Britain. He has published extensively in criminology and sociology journals, including *The Journal of Criminal Law and Criminology* and the *International Journal of Criminology and Penology*.